NOTTINGHAM FOREST
CHAMPIONS
1977/78

NOTTINGHAM FOREST
CHAMPIONS
1977/78

JOHN SHIPLEY

TEMPUS

This book is dedicated to my wife, Kate, and my two sons John and Peter. Also to the memory of the one and only Brian Clough, who sadly passed away on 20 September 2004

First published 2004

Tempus Publishing Limited
The Mill, Brimscombe Port,
Stroud, Gloucestershire, GL5 2QG
www.tempus-publishing.com

© John Shipley, 2004

The right of John Shipley to be identified as the Author
of this work has been asserted in accordance with the
Copyrights, Designs and Patents Act 1988.

British Library Cataloguing in Publication Data.
A catalogue record for this book is available from the British Library.

ISBN 0 7524 3366 0

Typesetting and origination by Tempus Publishing Limited
Printed and bound in Great Britain

Acknowledgements

I would like to say a big thank you to the following people for the assistance they have given to me during the production of this book. Particular thanks go to Rob Sharman, Holly Bennion and everyone at Tempus Publishing Group, without whom this book may not have ever been finished.

A huge extra-special thank you to Nottingham Forest Football Club for employing Brian Clough and winning all those lovely trophies.

To Brian Clough, a truly great man.

Everyone who has helped me, or loaned Forest memorabilia: Garry Birtles, Ray Whitehouse, Nick Bond, Mel Eves, Ken Sharpe.

My long-suffering proofreading wife Kate.

The *Express & Star*.

The *Birmingham Post & Mail*.

The *Nottingham Evening Post*.

The staff at the Birmingham City Library, Archives and Local Studies service.

The staff at the Nottingham Central Library, Archives and Local Studies service.

The staff at the Wolverhampton Archives and Local Studies service.

Photographic and other acknowledgements:

While every effort has been made to trace and acknowledge all copyright holders, we apologise for any errors or omissions. The author wishes to thank and acknowledge Empics for providing photographs and for permission to reproduce copyright material.

List of Matches

Football League First Division

Date	Competition	Forest's opponents	Home/Away	Score
20/08/77	League	Everton	A	3-1
23/08/77	League	Bristol City	H	1-0
27/08/77	League	Derby County	H	3-0
03/09/77	League	Arsenal	A	0-3
10/09/77	League	Wolverhampton Wanderers	A	3-2
17/09/77	League	Aston Villa	H	2-0
24/09/77	League	Leicester City	A	3-0
01/10/77	League	Norwich City	H	1-1
04/10/77	League	Ipswich Town	H	4-0
08/10/77	League	West Ham United	A	0-0
15/10/77	League	Manchester City	H	2-1
22/10/77	League	Queens Park Rangers	A	2-0
29/10/77	League	Middlesbrough	H	4-0
05/11/77	League	Chelsea	A	0-1
12/11/77	League	Manchester United	H	2-1
19/11/77	League	Leeds United	A	0-1
26/11/77	League	West Bromwich Albion	H	0-0
03/12/77	League	Birmingham City	A	2-0
10/12/77	League	Coventry City	H	2-1
17/12/77	League	Manchester United	A	4-0
26/12/77	League	Liverpool	H	1-1
28/12/77	League	Newcastle United	A	2-0
31/12/77	League	Bristol City	A	3-1
02/01/78	League	Everton	H	1-1
14/01/78	League	Derby County	A	0-0
21/01/78	League	Arsenal	H	2-0
04/02/78	League	Wolverhampton Wanderers	H	2-0
25/02/78	League	Norwich City	A	3-3

04/03/78	League	West Ham United	H	2-0
14/03/78	League	Leicester City	H	1-0
25/03/78	League	Newcastle United	H	2-0
29/03/78	League	Middlesbrough	A	2-2
01/04/78	League	Chelsea	H	3-1
05/04/78	League	Aston Villa	A	1-0
11/04/78	League	Manchester City	A	0-0
15/04/78	League	Leeds United	H	1-1
18/04/78	League	Queens Park Rangers	H	1-0
22/04/78	League	Coventry City	A	0-0
25/04/78	League	Ipswich Town	A	2-0
29/04/78	League	Birmingham City	H	0-0
02/05/78	League	West Bromwich Albion	A	2-2
04/05/78	League	Liverpool	A	0-0

Football League Cup:

Date	Round	Forest's opponents	Home/Away	Score
30/08/77	2	West Ham United	H	5-0
25/10/77	3	Notts County	H	4-0
29/11/77	4	Aston Villa	H	4-2
17/01/78	5	Bury	A	3-0
08/02/78	SF 1st Leg	Leeds United	A	3-1
22/02/78	SF 2nd Leg	Leeds United	H	4-2
18/03/78	Final	Liverpool	Wembley	0-0 aet
22/03/78	Final – Replay	Liverpool	Old Trafford	1-0

FA Cup:

Date	Round	Forest's opponents	Home/Away	Score
07/01/78	3	Swindon Town	H	4-1
31/01/78	4	Manchester City	H	2-1
18/02/78	5	Queens Park Rangers	A	1-1
27/02/78	5 – Replay	Queens Park Rangers	H	1-1
02/03/78	5 – 2nd Replay	Queens Park Rangers	H	3-1
11/03/78	6	West Bromwich Albion	A	0-2

Foreword
by Garry Birtles

I wanted to play for the mighty Reds from the time that I first kicked a football. When it actually happened, I had to pinch myself to make sure that I wasn't dreaming. I was one of those fortunate people who get to live their dream of playing professional football.

The game has given me so many wonderful memories. One of the best moments was hearing, when I was twenty and playing non-League football with Long Eaton while working as a carpet fitter, that Forest wanted to sign me. I was on cloud nine, as I was when I walked through the hallowed halls of the City Ground for the first time as a professional footballer. Meeting the legendary Brian Clough and Peter Taylor for the first time was daunting to say the least. They could be scary, but the 'Dynamic Duo' were the best management team in the business.

Words can't describe the thrill of making my League debut. Here I was, one of the Reds' loyal fans, steeped in the traditions of the City Ground, about to play for Forest's first team. Another great Forest memory was running out for the first time at Wembley on that thrilling League Cup-winning day in 1979, beating Southampton 3-2 and scoring two goals. The deafening noise as we emerged from the tunnel into a sea of red and white made it a very emotional moment. Bringing the trophy back to Nottingham and then repeating the experience with the European Cup was incredible. Being cheered by the people of your city, your family and friends, is magical to say the least. Scoring Forest's first ever goal in the European Cup and going on to become European Champions twice was the stuff of dreams.

Playing for your country is a great honour and I will never forget coming on as substitute for England in the 3-1 defeat of Argentina at Wembley, then being selected to start the game against Italy in the group stage of the European Championships – all wonderful memories.

It was a privilege to play for Brian Clough and Nottingham Forest Football Club; my nine wonderful years at the City Ground were my happiest in football. Happily, working for Century 106 FM and Sky television means that I'm still involved with the sport I love.

It's important to remember all of life's experiences, not in an over-the-top nostalgic way, but with a sense that the past will always have an enormous influence on the shape of the present and the future. Because of this I never tire of reading about Forest's history; I love it, and so can heartily recommend this book to you. In nostalgically chronicling the glorious history of the 1977/78 double-winning season John Shipley has captured the true spirit of the time as he takes the reader on a detailed and entertaining walk through Forest's first Championship-winning campaign, evoking so many wonderful memories which must never be forgotten. *Nottingham Forest, Champions 1977/78* is a timely souvenir of this wonderful achievement, and a fitting tribute to the memory of the great Brian Clough.

A true football fan, John's passion for the game shines through on every page. I'm sure you will enjoy it.

Introduction

Since joining the Football League in 1892, Nottingham Forest Football Club had strived to win the coveted League Championship. However, aside from a season of near-success in 1966/67, this ambition was not looking likely to be fulfilled. Well, not until the club's directors made what must be their best ever signing – Brian Clough.

Nottingham Forest had been relegated from the First Division at the end of season 1971/72, and there they had languished, hoping that one day a saviour would appear. Their prayers were answered when the saviour finally arrived. His name was Brian Clough. Clough was appointed manager of the club on 6 January 1975, following his unhappy and brief experience at Leeds United. In his first full season, Cloughie consolidated and Forest finished in eighth position in the Second Division. The team was beginning to take shape, playing some nice football, and becoming harder to beat; things were looking decidedly better for the Reds. July 1976 saw the arrival at the City Ground of Peter Taylor as assistant manager. The 'Dynamic Duo' that had achieved so much in their time together at Forest's deadly rivals from the other side of the M1 motorway were reunited once again. The pair set out to create a team capable of challenging for the game's top honours, and boy did they achieve this.

Their first trophy was the 1976/77 Anglo-Scottish Cup, won when Forest beat Orient in a two-legged final: 1-1 away, and 4-0 at home. However, the real breakthrough came at the end of that hard-fought season, when Forest managed to reach third place (thanks largely to a stuttering end to Bolton's season) and achieve automatic promotion back to the top flight. A reasonably small but strong squad had now to prepare for a season against the very best in English football. Clough and Taylor's solid looking team proved to be only three players short of fantastic.

What happened in season 1977/78 was the stuff of dreams, as Forest began an era of trophy-winning that was beyond the wildest flights of fantasy for even their most loyal fans, and for football pundits throughout the country. This was the second time that the Clough-Taylor partnership had taken over a Second Division club that was going nowhere, and within a relatively short time, turned them into Champions of the Football League. At Forest, they became masters of the Football League Cup, winning it four times, then attained the ultimate accolade of becoming European Champions, not once, but twice. It certainly wasn't luck – they were the tops.

This book is a diarised account of each game played in that epic 1977/78 season, when Nottingham Forest won their first League Championship, plus the Football League Cup. A 'double' to be proud of, and a season to remember.

Nottingham Forest 1977/78

1977 was a year packed with controversy. Among the more prominent events was the tearing up of the Wembley goalposts by a horde of overly exuberant Scottish fans following the Scots' 2-1 defeat of England on 4 June. This was England's final game before jetting off for a three-match tour of South America. England's highly unpopular and seemingly paranoid manager, 'dithering' Don Revie (as he had been christened by some press wag), baffled most sports-lovers by announcing his intention to travel to Helsinki to watch Italy play the Finns, rather than to Rio with his team. The truth later emerged that he had ended up in Dubai to finalise a reported £340,000, four-year deal to take over the United Arab Emirates side. Reputedly Revie even asked the FA to pay up the remaining two years of his contract, on the grounds that he thought he was about to be sacked. Events came to a head on 12 July, when Revie finally resigned. Revie out – Clough in, was the popular sentiment. In the wake of the Revie saga, rumours linking Brian Clough to the England job continued to worry Forest fans. Thus on Tuesday 16 August, the Forest faithful were pleased to hear that fifty-four-year-old Ron Greenwood was considering the FA's offer to succeed Revie as England manager, albeit on a temporary basis. Greenwood accepted the post the next day – the day Elvis Presley died. On 18 August, the FA announced that they were charging Don Revie with bringing the game into disrepute. FA secretary Ted Croker stated that Revie was in breach of the five-year, £25,000-a-year contract that he had signed with them.

As the start of the domestic season approached, the game was still facing a potential crisis of an even more epic proportion, as those that played the game continued to be at odds with those who ran it. At the Annual General Meeting of the Football League in July, the League chairmen voted to reject the proposed changes to the players' freedom of contract. With the negotiations at an impasse, the threat of disruption was now very real indeed. The simmering discontent of players with their lot, particularly with regard to the freedom of contract issue, continued to fester in a dispute that threatened to shake English football to its very core. Player discontent was not a new issue, it had been around since the first time that footballers realised they were part of the entertainment industry, and therefore should be paid accordingly. Matters had previously come to a head in 1960 when Jimmy Hill, he of beard and pointy chin fame, led the PFA in a long-running dispute with the Football League over the maximum wage and terms of contract. In 1960, the maximum wage was £20 per week in the season, and £17 in the summer. The widely held view among footballers and their union was that they were being exploited by their clubs. This was a time of great turmoil in English football. The tension between players and their clubs seemed impossible to overcome. The purse-holding directors of football clubs had always had complete control over their players, paying them a pittance by comparison to many other forms of entertainment, and preventing them from moving to a club of their choice on the expiry of their contract. Most of the players had simply had enough. PFA chairman Hill called it a 'slave contract' and a change was needed sooner rather than later.

With a strike only days away, the Football League finally backed down, and on 9 January 1961, the maximum wage was abolished. The League, however, steadfastly refused to budge on the issue of players' contracts. England inside forward George Eastham's contract with Newcastle ended and he wanted to join Arsenal, but his club refused to allow this. Faced with this dilemma he decided to challenge the legitimacy of his contract in court, arguing that it was a restraint of trade. Three days before the footballers' strike, which was still scheduled for 21 January 1961, the League capitulated. An agreement was reached to abandon the regulations that effectively tied a player to one club for life unless they wanted to transfer him. Eastham's PFA-backed challenge regarding his contract eventually went to the High Court, who ruled in his favour. Many chairmen thought, or maybe hoped, that this problem had gone away for good, but it hadn't, and now reared its head again sixteen years later.

In July 1977 professional footballers in the East Midlands pledged their full support for any action recommended by the Executive Committee of the PFA (Professional Footballer's Association). Then on 18 August, only two days before the new 1977/78 season was scheduled to get under way, more than 100 West Midlands footballers met PFA officials to discuss the breakdown in the negotiations over the issue of freedom of contract. At the end of a three-and-a-half-hour meeting the players gave the green light to the PFA proposals. Other meetings were planned in Manchester, Leeds and London over the course of the next three weeks. PFA chairman Derek Dougan and secretary Cliff Lloyd had earlier reached agreement with the Football League on this issue, but at the annual meeting of the League, it had been thrown out when fifteen clubs had voted against it. With the nation's footballers in favour of taking industrial action, and notifying the PFA of their support for this unparalleled step, the staging of any games on 20 August began to seem unlikely. Finally, and almost at the eleventh hour, the PFA secured an 'in principle' compromise, in which the League promised to outline the details of a change in the freedom of contract section of players' contracts. The problem was that this would not be forthcoming until later in the season. It was only on this basis that the season got under way.

In addition to all this upheaval, the usual pre-season manager's merry-go-round had seen six new faces in the top flight: Dave Sexton at Manchester United; Ronnie Allen at West Bromwich Albion; Ken Shellito at Chelsea; Frank Sibley at QPR; John Neal at Middlesbrough, and Frank McLintock at Leicester. But what of Nottingham Forest, and their return to the top division? How would they fare?

Soon after his appointment to the job of manager, Brian Clough began to assemble his team. In February 1975, he raided his previous club, Leeds, to sign John O'Hare and John McGovern, paying much less than when he had bought them from Derby. Two of his old dependable players were back under his wing. John Robertson and Martin O'Neill, both discontented under the previous incumbent Allan Brown, were reinstated to the first team. Next to join was the widely experienced full-back Frank Clark, who was secured on a free transfer from Newcastle in July 1975. Colin Barrett was signed from Manchester City in March 1976. Cloughie's old partner Peter Taylor came on board in July 1976. Shortly afterwards in September 1976, striker Peter Withe was purchased from Birmingham City, and in October 1976, ex-England and Liverpool pivot, Larry Lloyd, was bought from Coventry City. In July 1977, in came hardman striker/defender Kenny Burns from Birmingham

City. They joined former apprentices, goalkeepers John Middleton and Chris Woods, full-back Viv Anderson, and striker Tony Woodcock, plus the versatile and ever-dependable Ian Bowyer, who had been signed from Leyton Orient by Dave MacKay in October 1973. This then was the group of players that formed the nucleus of Clough and Taylor's team. Peter Shilton was signed from Stoke in September 1977, and in the same month, Archie Gemmill arrived from Derby County, with Leicester-born Dave Needham joining from QPR in December 1977, to add depth to the defence.

Forest's playing style under Clough was both simple and effective. A strong well-marshalled defence epitomised their marvellous teamwork, their passing was accurate and patient. In goal, after the first few games, Peter Shilton was outstandingly acrobatic, and in front of him was the solid and often quite scary pairing of Burns and Lloyd, plus in the second half of the season, Dave Needham. All were solid in the air and good on the ground, and ably supported by full-backs Anderson, Barrett and Clark. In the middle of the park, O'Neill covered the right-hand side, with the brilliant Robertson on the left supplying lots of ammunition, and in the centre, the ball-winning McGovern, Bowyer and later Gemmill provided the creativity. Up front, Withe and Woodcock chased and harried as well as scoring goals.

There is no doubt that Clough and Taylor's team included many fine individual players, but it was the way the blend worked together that made them extra special. This is what made the Reds a Championship-winning side in 1977/78. Yes, they were fortunate where injuries were concerned, but nothing should be taken away from their achievements because of this. They were a team to be proud of. A great team spirit was forged. Everyone in the squad knew their job, as well as what to expect from their colleagues. Clough had them all playing to their strengths. Apart from John Middleton, who played only the first five League games, a mere fifteen players were used in the League and FA Cup campaigns, plus one, Chris Woods, for the Football League Cup games, to bring the overall total number of players used in the three 1977/78 domestic competitions to seventeen. Surely, one of the fewest ever in a Championship-winning season, which of course with Forest's success in the League Cup, was also a 'double.'

So, that's the background, now let's move on to the game-by-game diary of Nottingham Forest's marvellous 1977/78 season. In 1977/78, many teams employed either a 4-4-2 or a 4-3-3 formation largely depending upon how attack-minded the manager was. Of course, the degree of talent of the team or their opposition would also determine the formation on the park, so there was still a fair amount of flexibility. In some teams, the shirt numbers meant nothing in terms of the traditional playing positions. Throughout this book, in the interests of clarity, I have listed the players sequentially by shirt number for all the team line-ups.

Forest's first game of the season saw them travel to the city of Liverpool to play the Toffees of Everton.

EVERTON v. NOTTINGHAM FOREST

Football League First Division, Goodison Park **Date:** Saturday 20 August 1977
Attendance: 38,001 **Referee:** Mr K. Stiles (Barnsley)

After just about managing to scrape promotion from the Second Division, courtesy of a Wolves victory over Bolton, and having made just one pre-season signing, Forest got off to a winning start with this emphatic victory over the previous season's League Cup runners-up.

Gordon Lee's Everton were fancied to do well in 1977/78, having finished in ninth place the previous season and having only lost the League Cup final to Aston Villa 3-2 after extra time in the second replay. The Toffees had also reached the semi-finals of the FA Cup, losing to Liverpool in a replay after drawing the first game, so they looked a strong side. They had a solid defence and a creative midfield, although for today's game they would be without Martin Dobson and unsettled Bruce Rioch. Up front, the Toffees would be missing their powerful striker, big Bob Latchford, but would still pose a serious threat through Forest old boy Duncan McKenzie, who had arrived at Everton via Leeds and Belgian club Anderlecht. Making his debut in the Everton goal was George Wood, signed from Blackpool for £140,000, and Dave Thomas, a £200,000 capture from QPR. For Forest, new signing Kenny Burns would play wearing number six.

Against all expectations, except those in Nottingham, goals from Peter Withe (whose broken nose had threatened to keep him out of this game), John Robertson and Martin O'Neill sank the home side without trace.

Forest began the game brightly. Burns sent over a free-kick that former Blackpool 'keeper Wood did well to pluck out of the air before the ball could reach Withe. However, it was Everton who got the early upper hand, running Forest ragged in the first quarter of an hour. Mike Pejic made progress down the left, which Larry Lloyd came to meet. The ex-Stoke full-back managed to force the ball through to Darracott, who controlled the ball neatly, before powering in a vicious thirty-yard shot, which narrowly missed the angle of the goal. Burns and Lloyd, together with McGovern, combined to bring some degree of calmness to the Forest defence and midfield, stubbornly resisting Everton's early pressure. Burns heading away a number of crosses and free-kicks, Lloyd and McGovern making many successful tackles.

Forest then spurned a great chance to take the lead. Tony Woodcock was on the receiving end of a scything tackle from Kenyon just outside Everton's penalty area. Robertson cheekily threaded a pass to Bowyer, but the ginger-haired midfielder lost control before he was able to get in a strike at goal. During this period of the game, it looked as if Everton's McKenzie had gone absent without leave. In their next attack, a Thomas corner bobbled around menacingly before Lloyd swung his boot to clear the danger and now it was the Reds on the attack. Ian Bowyer cut inside from the right and sent in a stinging left-footed drive that was always swinging away from its intended target.

Suddenly former Forest ace McKenzie came alive. Showing his class by out-thinking big Larry, who must have thought he was in control of the situation, Duncan squared a clever ball across the

---

Everton 1 **Nottingham Forest 3**

Pearson (44) Withe (20), Robertson (38),
O'Neill (77)

EVERTON V. NOTTINGHAM FOREST

goal area that Frank Clark managed to reach first to prevent an Everton goal. Then McKenzie latched on to a back-header from Pearson to whizz in a right-footed screamer that was only inches past the post. At the other end Robertson was causing all kinds of danger for the Everton defence, sending over a series of dangerous centres. Most were cleared with difficulty; however, one delicate cross reached Bowyer, whose first-time volley beat the diving Wood all ends up, but which Kenyon somehow managed to head clear. Surely a goal must come soon.

In the twentieth minute, the Reds won a corner from which Peter Withe scored Forest's first goal of the season. The ball dropped at the near post, and Withe leapt high to power his header into the top corner of the net. Now it was Forest's turn to dominate the game, as they attacked in force. It was as if that single goal had blown away any lingering doubts that they hadn't any right to be there. Wood parried Bowyer's goal-bound effort and was pleased to grab the ball at the second attempt.

On thirty-eight minutes, Woodcock forced a corner on the right, which the young Forest forward took himself. He whipped over a swerving centre, which Wood made a mess of gathering, the ball spun off a defender to Robbo who made no mistake with a cracking shot that went in off the far post.

A minute before the interval Everton pulled one back. Pejic's cross from the left was headed down by Lyons for Jim Pearson to blast past Middleton. So far, so good; 2-1 up at half-time was fine.

After the break, Forest resumed their attack on the home side's goal, Robertson again beating Jones comfortably, but this time Wood, who had not had the happiest of debuts, made a good catch. After Forest had gone close with good efforts by McGovern and Woodcock that had Wood struggling, Everton manager Gordon Lee set on Goodlass to replace Terry Darracott.

Forest's unrelenting pressure brought a third goal in the seventy-seventh minute. Robbo again left Jones for dead and the mercurial winger cut in to unleash a powerful drive that Wood could only palm away into the path of the onrushing O'Neill who smacked the ball into the net from close range. The third goal knocked the stuffing out of Everton and they never managed to mount any further serious attacks. The Reds were good value for their 3-1 victory.

A great start indeed, and one in the eye for the doubters. Next up was the home game against Bristol City, who had been promoted to the First Division the year before Forest.

Sadly for **John Middleton**, Brian Clough wanted the very best 'keeper in the land, and so he lost his place to Peter Shilton, and was subsequently sold to Derby in September 1977 as part of the deal that saw Archie Gemmill join the Reds. John was born in Lincolnshire on 24 December 1956, signing apprenticeship forms with Forest in June 1973, and professional forms in November 1974. He made his debut on 19 October 1974 in the game against West Bromwich Albion, and played a big part in Forest's 1975/76 promotion-winning team, and in the 1977 Anglo-Scottish Cup success, going on to make 90 first-team appearances in the League, before moving to the Baseball Ground. John played for England Youth and won 3 caps for England Under-21s. Sadly, a shoulder injury forced him to retire from the game in May 1980.

Everton: Wood, Jones, Pejic, Lyons, Kenyon, Higgins, King, Darracott (Goodlass), Pearson, McKenzie, Thomas.
Nottingham Forest: Middleton, Anderson, Clark, McGovern, Lloyd, Burns, O'Neill, Bowyer, Withe, Woodcock, Robertson. Sub: Barrett

The Nottingham Forest team pre-season.

Nottingham Forest v. Bristol City

Football League First Division, City Ground
Attendance: 21,743

Date: Tuesday 23 August 1977
Referee: Mr A.F. Jenkins (Scunthorpe)

Bristol City had opened their League campaign with a 3-2 home defeat at the hands of Wolves, a game of three penalties, but only two for City. Right-back Donnie Gillies had suffered a knee injury in the Wolves game and would miss this match, his place being taken by Gerry Sweeney. The further bad news for the Robins was that striker Chris Garland's stiff neck had failed to respond to treatment, and so manager Alan Dicks brought in eighteen-year-old former England Schoolboys striker Kevin Mabbutt.

The Reds came out all guns blazing, but this strong City side that had finished fifth from bottom the year before stubbornly refused to lie down. Eventually, Peter Withe stuck the ball away with a great header to make it two wins out of two. City's defensive general was none other than Norman ('bite your legs') Hunter. The ex-Leeds and England man was on top form all night, reading the game superbly, plugging any gaps that appeared, and heading away every ball that came his way, except of course when our Pete finally outjumped him and his mates in the eighty-second minute. Because of the close attentions of right-back Gerry Sweeney, this was turning out to be one of Robbo's quieter games. However, it was when he switched to the right flank that Forest's goal came. Ex-Liverpool player Peter Cormack, operating as an extra left-back, brought him down, and when the free-kick came over Withe rose magnificently above the Robins defenders to power the ball past John Shaw. The Robins had created a couple of chances, the best of which came two minutes after the hour mark. Tom Ritchie and Kevin Mabbutt exchanged passes in a neat double act, before the former whipped in a snarling effort that slammed against the foot of the post. Apart from this, City appeared to be playing for a draw, packing their defence in an effort to stifle Nottingham Forest's creativity.

Forest continued to bash away for most of the game, each attack floundering on the defensive rock that was Norman Hunter, although twice Bowyer got into a great position, only to squander each chance. The first came when he dallied too long before shooting, and the ball spun off a defender for a corner. From Woodcock's kick, Larry Lloyd headed down to Bowyer who missed the target from almost point-blank range. Then eight minutes from time, Robertson skinned the doubled-up full-backs, and sidestepped Hunter, before being fouled by Cormack. Robbo drifted his free-kick into the danger area, and the rest was academic as Peter Withe notched his second goal of the new season. Another two points safely in the bag. Kenny Burns was outstanding, producing a performance that justified his reported £150,000 price tag.

Well now, as they say in these parts, 'bring on the sheep'. Forest had waited five years to have another crack at their near-neighbours. The year the Reds had been relegated to the Second Division had been humiliating enough, but worse still, Derby, under Clough and Taylor, had won the 1971/72 League title. And of course, Derby had repeated this feat under Dave MacKay in 1974/75, who ironically had left the City Ground to take over at Derby when Cloughie left in 1973.

Nottingham Forest 1
Withe (82)

Bristol City 0

Forest goalscorer Peter Withe.

Nottingham Forest: Middleton, Anderson, Clark, McGovern, Lloyd, Burns, O'Neill, Bowyer, Withe, Woodcock, Robertson. Sub: Barrett

Bristol City: Shaw, Sweeney, Merrick (Mann), Gow, Collier, Hunter, Tainton, Ritchie, Mabbutt, Cormack, Whitehead.

Nottingham Forest v. Derby County

Football League First Division, City Ground **Date:** Saturday 27 August 1977
Attendance : 28,807 **Referee:** Mr K.H. Burns (Stourbridge)

Forest fans were sent home delighted to have thumped their near-neighbours by three clear goals. A brace for Peter Withe and one from Robertson sealed a fabulous victory over Tommy Docherty's side. In the first minute, Forest might have taken the lead. Roy McFarland pushed Peter Withe near the byline and from the resultant free-kick Robertson forced Colin Boulton in the Derby goal to stretch to punch the ball away, and Gerry Daly booted it clear. The Rams, without Charlie George, did fashion an early attempt on goal which had Middleton scrambling to pounce on the ball. A needless corner, given away by Burns, was whipped in by David Nish. Larry Lloyd powerfully headed the ball clear, but only as far as Daly, who cracked in a shot that Middleton did well to catch under the bar. Then winger Bill Hughes volleyed well wide, before Burns and McGovern had good efforts blocked, and O'Neill had put a good chance over the bar. The game swung from end to end with both sets of midfielders prompting chances that were kept out by some solid defending. Steve Powell was booked for hauling back Ian Bowyer, then Burns took a nasty knock to the ankle, which needed treatment before he could resume.

Just past the half-hour mark, Peter Withe thumped in a great shot to put the Reds one up, and maintain his goal-a-game start to the season. Viv Anderson broke up a Derby Ram-raid, and powered forward, eventually forcing a corner. Woodcock swung over his usual inswinger, but Boulton beat Lloyd to the ball; unfortunately for the Rams the ball fell to the Forest centre forward, who volleyed the ball inches inside the post with his left foot. That's the way it stayed until half-time.

In the build-up to another surging run that earned Robertson a corner, Roy McFarland stretched too far, straining his hamstring. The Derby captain was obviously in pain, and when he was helped from the field, it looked unlikely that he would be able to continue. Sure enough, substitute Ron Webster came on, in a Derby reshuffle that saw Powell take over at centre half. Both goalkeepers continued to make good saves, particularly the busier of the two, Colin Boulton, whose agility kept out Robertson. Archie Gemmill, as tireless as ever, fired over, as did Daly and Kevin Hector. In the sixty-first minute, Woodcock had the ball in the Rams' net when he raced on to a neat pass from McGovern to place his accurate shot past Boulton. The Derby hands went aloft, as did the linesman's flag and the goal was chalked off for offside.

Forest were powering forward at every opportunity and it seemed only a matter of time before they would get a second goal. It came in the sixty-seventh minute, following a successful tackle on Woodcock by David Langan. The ball ran to O'Neill, whose perfect chip was knocked back to Withe by Robertson. The big number nine wasted no time in dispatching the ball into the net. Following a series of missed chances, the Reds got a well-deserved third goal. This time it was Robertson who grabbed it. O'Neill crossing for the winger to let rip with a well-placed shot. Three

Nottingham Forest 3 **Derby County 0**
Withe 2 (31, 67), Robertson (78)

Brian Clough pre-season 1977/78.

wins on the trot took Forest to the top of the table, even better than the hardiest Red had hoped for. Forest were now the only club with three wins out of three.

Table after the first three League games:

	PLD	W	D	L	F	A	PTS
Forest	**3**	**3**	**0**	**0**	**7**	**1**	**6**
Liverpool	3	2	1	0	6	1	5
Man Utd	3	2	1	0	6	2	5
Man City	3	2	1	0	5	1	5
Wolves	3	2	1	0	5	3	5
Coventry	3	2	0	1	6	4	4

Now it was time for a break from the League; the Hammers were coming to town to play Forest in the League Cup.

Nottingham Forest: Middleton, Anderson, Clark, McGovern, Lloyd, Burns, O'Neill, Bowyer, Withe, Woodcock, Robertson. Sub: Curran

Derby County: Boulton, Langan, Nish, Daly G., McFarland (Webster), Todd, Powell, Gemmill, Hales, Hector, Hughes.

NOTTINGHAM FOREST v. WEST HAM UNITED

Football League Cup, second round, City Ground   **Date:** Tuesday 30 August 1977
Attendance : 18,224   **Referee:** Mr Dennis Turner (Cannock)

For the second time in three days, Forest fans left the City Ground in an ecstatic mood, this time after seeing their team wallop the Hammers by five clear goals, to cruise into the third round.

Unchanged Forest set about their task with much gusto, turning in a powerful display of attacking football. Apart from a few individualistic moments, West Ham were a bit ordinary to say the least, and were certainly no match for a strong-looking Forest side that literally steamrollered over them with not an ounce of compassion. It was boys against men. The disappointingly low gate was treated to a fine display of attacking football. Twenty-four-year-old John Robertson was at his teasing best as he constantly tormented the Hammers' defence with his brilliant runs along the left touchline. Not long after the game kicked off, Robbo smashed in a twenty-five-yard shot that had Mervyn Day clawing at thin air; unfortunately the ball missed its intended target. Then in the fourth minute, Middleton had to get down smartly, the young 'keeper diving to his right to keep out a fine solo effort from Bryan 'Pop' Robson.

The goal scoring fun began five minutes later when Lloyd controlled the ball well before bringing it out of defence to send Robbo away on the left. Over came the customary accurate cross, which was gathered by Woodcock, who turned his man brilliantly before sliding the ball across goal for Martin O'Neill to rifle home. Middleton was again in action when he had to be quick to snuff out a dangerous situation after Larry Lloyd's intended clearance bounced into the path of Alan Taylor. But five minutes before the half-hour mark, the Reds created another opening. Again, Robertson was the instigator, beating the full-back to whip the ball over. Ian Bowyer met it perfectly to head past Mervyn Day. Frank Lampard earned himself a booking when he brought down Robertson. The half-time score was 2-0 to Forest.

At the start of the second half, Taylor worked himself into a good position, but his rising centre cleared the inrushing Robson by an inch or two. However, that was pretty much the sum total of the Hammers' endeavours. West Ham 'keeper Day gifted Forest a third goal when he completely botched his near-post positioning, allowing Woodcock to beat him, the ball squeezing into the net through the tightest of gaps; the young striker's first of the season. In the seventy-eighth minute Peter Withe put Forest into an unassailable lead, darting in to head Robbo's cross past the stunned Mervyn Day from close in. Then in the eighty-fifth minute Robbo reversed a great ball into the run of Bowyer, who hit a tremendous shot into the corner of the net.

Beyond doubt, the Reds could, and should, have scored more. Both central defenders went close, and Withe's all-round display might have brought him a hat-trick on another day. This was still a fabulous performance by Forest; a nice long League Cup run would be very acceptable. The chant at the City Ground could have been 'We're forever bursting bubbles.'

The lads returned to League action 'wiv a trip darn saarf'.

Nottingham Forest 5   **West Ham United 0**
  O'Neill (9), Bowyer 2 (25, 85),
  Woodcock (65), Withe (78)

Nottingham Forest v. West Ham United

Ian Bowyer.

Nottingham Forest: Middleton, Anderson, Clark, McGovern, Lloyd, Burns, O'Neill, Bowyer, Withe, Woodcock, Robertson. Sub: Curran

West Ham United: Day, Lampard, Brush (Otulakowski), Pike, Green, Lock, Taylor, Robson B., Radford, Curbishley, Devonshire.

ARSENAL v. NOTTINGHAM FOREST

Football League First Division, Highbury
Attendance: 40,810

Date: Saturday 3 September 1977
Referee: Mr R.C. Challis (Tonbridge)

The wheels came off temporarily at Highbury as the Gunners fired straight and true, Frank Stapleton getting them off to a dream start. From Sammy Nelson's cross, the Irishman rose high above the Forest defenders to loop a great header over Middleton into the net. Arsenal kept up the pressure, and Powling went close from around twenty-five yards. Left-winger Graham Rix was causing a lot of problems for Viv Anderson. Then Ross's thunderbolt was deflected for a corner after Powling had wasted a good opportunity. Forest's first meaningful attack saw Robertson put his centre into the side netting to the relief of big Pat Jennings. The Irish 'keeper was eagerly gobbling up every ball that Forest sent into his penalty area, confirming his reputation as one the League's finest. By half-time, Forest's defenders knew they had been in one heck of a battle. It had certainly been a bit of a backs-to-the-wall effort for the first forty-five minutes. One-nil was not a true reflection of what the Gunners deserved, but at least Forest still had a chance to get something from the game.

Unfortunately, the second half continued much as the first, with Arsenal constantly attacking, and Forest's beleaguered defence becoming more and more punch drunk. Stapleton thumped in a shot that cannoned off Middleton, and then Brady put a free-kick wide. Ian Bowyer earned a little respite with a free-kick. Robertson floated over a high ball that Jennings punched clear with consummate ease. O'Neill subsequently spoiled a good situation by spooning his shot well wide. Forest appeared to have recovered a little of their normal composure and forced Jennings into making a double save after Nelson's error had allowed Woodcock to whip in a hard shot. The Irishman blocked his effort and then had to scramble across his goal to prevent O'Neill from putting the loose ball into the Gunners' net. On the hour Forest's hopes were shattered when Stapleton collected a rebound following a corner by Powling to rifle home a fierce shot into the corner of the net, and as if that wasn't bad enough, the Gunners went further ahead nine minutes later. This time it was a hotly disputed penalty that did the damage. Stapleton fell over when Burns challenged him for the ball, the linesman thought he had seen an infringement and drew it to the referee's attention; Mr Challis hadn't seen anything wrong. The linesman was adamant and the ref pointed to the spot; Burns was not happy, he felt that Stapleton had dived. For a fleeting moment, the situation looked like it might turn into an ugly incident, bringing to mind Kenny's previous reputation for trouble. Fortunately referee Challis calmed everyone down, booking Burns, and Brady slammed the penalty past Middleton.

Jennings kept out a good effort from Ian Bowyer, after the same player had crashed a thunderbolt against the foot of the post which bounced agonisingly the wrong way, going out for a goal kick. Then Middleton got in on the goalkeeping act with excellent saves from Super Mac and Frank Stapleton. During the game Frank Clark received a bad knock and had to be substituted, Colin Barrett coming on at left-back for his first taste of League action. Following televised incidents from the game, Cloughie is reputed to have imposed fines on Larry Lloyd and Kenny Burns.

Arsenal 3
  Stapleton 2 (3, 60),
  Brady (penalty 69)

Nottingham Forest 0

Colin Barrett.

Born in Stockport on 3 August 1952, versatile defender **Colin Barrett** was signed by Forest from Manchester City for a fee reported to be £30,000, in March 1976, making his debut on 13 May 1976 in the game against Fulham. Barrett was equally at home in any of the defensive or midfield positions, although most pundits regarded left-back as his best position.

He was the scorer of the fabulous goal in the European Cup tie with Liverpool that sealed a great win against the two-time Euro Champs, and made 69 League appearances for Forest, including 5 as substitute, scoring 4 League goals. In June 1980, he was sold to Swindon Town.

ARSENAL v. NOTTINGHAM FOREST

The table after four games:

	PLD	W	D	L	F	A	PTS
Man City	4	3	1	0	9	1	7
Liverpool	4	3	1	0	7	1	7
Man U	4	3	1	0	7	2	7
Forest	**4**	**3**	**0**	**1**	**7**	**4**	**6**
Wolves	4	2	2	0	5	3	6
Ipswich	4	2	2	0	2	0	6

Losing the Arsenal game not only knocked the Reds off top spot, but it shoved them down into fourth place. Bottom of the League were Newcastle United, and one place above them, Derby County.

England Under-21s walloped Norway 6-0 at Brighton on 6 September 1977, with Forest's John Middleton playing in goal. The full England side met Switzerland in a friendly at Wembley on 7 September 1977, in a 0-0 draw. The England team was: Clemence, Neal, Cherry, McDermott, Watson, Hughes (Capt.), Keegan, Channon (Hill), Francis, Kennedy, Callaghan (Wilkins). Scotland were beaten 1-0 in East Germany and in further domestic news Alf Ramsey was appointed caretaker manager at Birmingham City on 8 September.

Forest's next trip would take them to the West Midlands for the first time this season. Their opponents would be Wolves, Second Division Champions the season that Forest were promoted. Here was a good chance for Forest to gauge just how much progress they had made. The breaking team news was that terms had been agreed for the transfer of Peter Shilton from Stoke to Forest for £270,000. Brian Clough had increased his initial offer from £240,000 and so the move was on. It was hoped that the deal would be completed by Monday, and that Shilton would be presented to the City Ground faithful before Liam O'Kane's testimonial on the Monday evening, although there were still a few minor financial problems to be resolved. Shilton had joined Stoke City from Leicester City for £340,000 in November 1974.

Arsenal: Jennings, Rice, Nelson, Powling, O'Leary, Young, Brady, Ross, MacDonald, Stapleton, Rix. Sub: Price
Nottingham Forest: Middleton, Anderson, Clark (Barrett), McGovern, Lloyd, Burns, O'Neill, Bowyer, Withe, Woodcock, Robertson.

WOLVERHAMPTON WANDERERS V. NOTTINGHAM FOREST

Football League First Division, Molineux
Attendance: 24,662

Date: Saturday 10 September 1977
Referee: Mr G. Noland (Stockport)

At Molineux, Forest beat a patched-up Wolves side to confirm their position as a force to be reckoned with. Frank Clark had not recovered from the hamstring injury he received at Arsenal and so Colin Barrett got his first start of the season. Wolves had been well and truly stuffed in their mid-week League Cup tie by Second Division Luton Town at Molineux, and for this West versus East Midlands clash, would be without powerful striker Steve Kindon. Apparently, the big number ten had injured his foot in a bizarre cycling accident earlier in the week.

As usual, Forest were well-organised from defence to attack, and undoubtedly won the aerial battle of Molineux with far more ease than Wolves would have liked. For three-quarters of this game, Kenny Burns and Larry Lloyd dominated John Richards and Alan Sunderland, and with the rest of the home side playing well below par, it was maybe a bit too easy for the Reds. For some unfathomable reason, Wolves' only attacking idea was to constantly hit high balls into the Forest penalty area. The first real chance came in the eighteenth minute when, with Phil Parkes slow to come off his line, Peter Withe once again rose above the defence to head the ball home from a Burns free-kick near the halfway line. Oddly, considering the possession that Forest were enjoying, that's the way it stayed at half-time.

The second half began in similar fashion, but then the visitors' calm was dented slightly by Willie Carr who smacked in a good fifty-first minute effort that in the end didn't really trouble the unruffled John Middleton. On sixty-four minutes, Forest scored again, Ian Bowyer leaping to nod the ball past Phil Parkes to double Forest's tally, and eight minutes later Tony Woodcock looked to have wrapped up the points with a deft header. Withe crossed from the right and the young striker guided it superbly into Wanderers' net. Forest eased off the gas a little, and who could blame them? After all, they were three goals up with only eighteen minutes to play. But, football is a funny old game isn't it?

Wolves, encouraged by substitute Norman Bell, stormed back and got a goal almost immediately following Forest's third. Right-back Geoff Palmer flighted in a quality cross which John Richards won at the far post, heading the ball down for Norman Bell to thump past Middleton. Ten minutes later the referee pointed to the spot when Lloyd fouled Richards: penalty to Wolves. Up stepped Steve Daley to send the ball past Middleton and set up a frenetic end to the game. Fortunately, for Forest, Wolves couldn't find the hat let alone pull a rabbit from it and so the Reds took the points.

This was Wolves' first League defeat of the season; they were obviously missing the power and pace of the injured Steve Kindon. From their point of view, to lose three headed goals showed a lack of concentration on the part of a number of their defenders. Having said that, the scoreline definitely flattered Wolves.

Wolverhampton Wanderers 2
Bell (72), Daley (penalty 82)

Nottingham Forest 3
Withe (18), Bowyer (64),
Woodcock (72)

WOLVERHAMPTON WANDERERS v. NOTTINGHAM FOREST

Table:

	PLD	W	D	L	F	A	PTS
Man City	5	4	1	0	12	2	9
Liverpool	5	4	1	0	9	1	9
Forest	**5**	**4**	**0**	**1**	**10**	**6**	**8**
WBA	5	3	1	1	10	6	7
Man U	5	3	1	1	8	5	7
Leeds	5	3	2	1	9	8	6

Newcastle United remained bottom with 2 points, and one place above them with the same points total were Derby County.

On Monday 12 September, the Shilton transfer saga hit a new snag. A dispute over the payment of a £5,000 loyalty bonus reared its head. Shilton's claim was that he was entitled to this, and wanted it before agreeing to move. Stoke were adamant that the England goalkeeper hadn't qualified for the bonus and therefore refused to pay. Stoke manager George Eastham attempted to break the deadlock by asking if Forest would pay the £5,000. I wonder if the second word of the reply was 'off'?

On Monday night a Forest XI played a testimonial for Liam O'Kane against Leicester City at the City Ground. The result was a surprising 0-0 draw, watched by 5,190 fans, and refereed by Mr B. Martin of Keyworth. Forest's team, including guests was: Middleton, O'Kane, Barrett, McGovern, Burns, Todd, O'Neill, Gemmill, Withe, McKenzie, Robertson. Subs: Anderson, Bowyer, Lloyd. No Shilton! He was still with Stoke. On 14 September 1977, it was reported by the press that Stoke and England goalkeeper Peter Shilton had finally given up his claim to the £5,000 bonus that had been at the heart of the delay with his transfer, and joined Forest from Stoke City for £270,000. Now Clough had completed his rebuilding of the spine of his team. The strong backbone that he had always believed was necessary for any team aspiring to be successful was in place. Shilton would be in the Forest team to face Aston Villa on Saturday. Hu-perishin'-rray!

At a press conference, six West Midlands football clubs announced that they were steadfastly opposed to the principle of players' freedom of contract, and would vote against this proposal at next Monday's Football League extraordinary meeting.

On Friday 16 September twenty-nine-year-old T-Rex singer Marc Bolan was killed when the Mini Cooper being driven by his girlfriend Gloria Jones crashed into a tree.

Wolverhampton Wanderers: Parkes, Palmer, Daly, Daley, Parkin, McAlle, Patching, Carr, Richards, Todd (Bell), Sunderland.

Nottingham Forest: Middleton, Anderson, Barrett, McGovern, Lloyd, Burns, O'Neill, Bowyer, Withe, Woodcock, Robertson. Sub: O'Hare

Nottingham Forest v. Aston Villa

Football League First Division, City Ground
Attendance: 31,016

Date: Saturday 17 September 1977
Referee: Mr A. Porter (Bolton)

Hard-running Forest crushed Aston Villa, but certainly didn't have to work overly hard to secure this victory. Their record buy, goalkeeper Peter Shilton, made his debut for Forest and was hardly troubled at any stage of the match. Frankly, Villa were poor so far as creativity was concerned. They showed no semblance of any kind of cohesion anywhere on the park. Their midfield were rushed in their work, and in attack, if that's not a complete misnomer, Brian Little and his colleagues were powder-puff soft, and certainly missed the authority and presence of Andy Gray.

Time after time, they were far too easily brushed off the ball by power-twins Larry Lloyd and Kenny Burns, only managing one shot between them all game. The contrast with the always-lively and dangerous Peter Withe and Tony Woodcock was immense. Having said all that, Villa couldn't be faulted for their work rate, they competed in most areas of the park. It just seemed that they played as individuals and not as a team.

Young Tony Woodcock had married his fiancée on the previous Sunday, and it was he that opened up the scoring for Forest in the fifth minute; his third of the season. Larry Lloyd started the move, his powerful run out of defence slicing through the Villa midfield. A neat pass put Withe away on the left, and although £200,000 former Everton defender Ken McNaught tried to force him wide, the number nine managed to send over a low cross to Woodcock. In one movement, the young Forest striker turned-on-a-tanner, before rifling his shot past Rimmer, the ball going into the net off the inside of the far post.

Early in the game, Carrodus was injured in a heavy challenge, and was clearly in some distress, which restricted his effectiveness. Villa just couldn't get going. Nor did they appear to have any answer to Robbo's surging runs down the left, the Scottish winger constantly proving to be a thorn in the side of John Gidman. In their next attack, Barrett, McGovern and Bowyer combined superbly in a move that ended with the latter sending a well-flighted cross, which the Villa defence were pleased to see cleared. Next, Bowyer chipped the ball up for Woodcock to nod into the penalty area, but before Withe could reach the ball, it was booted clear. Frank Carrodus, who was now moving much more comfortably, kept plugging away, but to no great effect. He did manage to reach a through ball from Leighton Phillips, but scooped his effort into the crowd. Soon after, a little bit of afters between Lloyd and Little might have got out of hand, but only ended up with big Larry wagging an accusing finger at the Villa striker.

It was all-out attack from Forest, and 'backs to the wall' desperate defending for Villa, with Shilton a virtual spectator. His teammates must have recognised this and occasionally played the ball back to him to prevent him becoming too bored. The England 'keeper did have one save to make in the fortieth minute, when, after Deehan had forced Barrett to concede a corner, Pete showed his class by comfortably catching the ball in the centre of his goal area.

Nottingham Forest 2
Woodcock (5), Robertson (89)

Aston Villa 0

Nottingham Forest v. Aston Villa

The second half was a repeat of the first forty-five minutes, with shots being blocked or saved by Rimmer. Somehow, Villa managed to hold out until one minute from full time, when Robbo wrapped it up for the Reds.

Table:

	PLD	W	D	L	F	A	PTS
Man City	6	4	2	0	13	3	10
Liverpool	6	4	2	0	10	2	10
Forest	**6**	**5**	**0**	**1**	**12**	**6**	**10**
WBA	6	3	2	1	12	8	8
Everton	6	3	1	2	11	6	7

Also on 7 points were Manchester United, Arsenal, Leeds, Coventry, Wolves and Ipswich.

Forty-eight hours after the Villa game, on Monday 19 September, the directors of all ninety-two Football League clubs met for an extraordinary meeting with the threat of the first ever footballers' strike hanging over their heads. The main topic of discussion was the contentious matter of players' freedom of contract, which had been rejected at a previous meeting. A number of Midland clubs opposed the acceptance of the proposals, worried about the potential anomalies within the proposed compensation system, where they felt that the amount payable to the selling club would be open to manipulation. Strike action was averted when the clubs voted to accept the proposals. The Football League clubs also changed their minds and agreed to allow sponsors' names to appear on shirts in games that were not televised.

Also on this day, ex-Leeds and England manager Don Revie was officially suspended by the Football Association and banned from any involvement in football under the jurisdiction of the FA until he returned to answer the charges of bringing the game into disrepute.

On Wednesday 21 September 1977, Martin O'Neill played for Northern Ireland alongside George Best in a World Cup qualifier against Iceland in Belfast. They won 2-0.

On Friday 23 September, it was announced that Derby County manager Tommy Docherty had agreed to the exchange-transfer of Archie Gemmill to Forest in a deal that would cost the Reds a £100,000 transfer fee, and see England Under-21 goalkeeper John Middleton cross the M1 to the Baseball Ground. Apparently, Docherty forced Gemmill to sign a written transfer request, and thus forfeit his cut of the deal worth a reputed £6,500.

Nottingham Forest: Shilton, Anderson, Barrett, McGovern, Lloyd, Burns, O'Neill, Bowyer, Withe, Woodcock, Robertson. Sub: O'Hare

Aston Villa: Rimmer, Gidman, Robson J., Phillips, McNaught, Mortimer, Deehan, Little, Cowans, Cropley, Carrodus. Sub: Smith

Leicester City v. Nottingham Forest

Football League First Division, Filbert Street
Attendance: 21,447

Date: Saturday 24 September 1977
Referee: Mr T. Mills (Barnsley)

The Foxes were well and truly hunted and dispatched in this one-sided East Midlands derby. With John O'Hare replacing the injured Peter Withe, the Reds stormed to the attack, their early pressure yielding an eighteenth minute goal. Martin O'Neill moved on to a neat pass on the left of the area and whipped in a fierce shot that goalkeeper Mark Wallington couldn't hang on to. Fortunately for the Irish winger the ball spun back to him and he was able to slot it into the net with ease at the second attempt.

The remainder of the first half turned out to be a bit of a scrappy affair, with Forest doing most of the attacking, goal attempts coming from every one of the forwards. Leicester's main outlet was that great rock 'n' roller Frank Worthington; however, only a couple of half-chances came his way.

The second half saw the Foxes try to take the game to the Reds. Worthington cracked in a twenty-five-yard drive that failed to trouble Shilton; this was only Frank's and Leicester's second real effort on goal. The flow of the play wasn't helped by a succession of free-kicks that certainly disrupted the game. However, it was obvious that Forest were the least troubled, and always looked like they might add to their lead. Sure enough in the sixty-third minute, Tony Woodcock was on hand to score for the third successive game. Robertson once again left Whitworth for dead to send over another perfect cross. Up rose John O'Hare to flick the ball on to the far post where Woodcock forced the ball past Wallington.

It wasn't long before Forest almost went three up. This time it was Ian Bowyer, who jinked his way into the penalty area past a couple of fairly static Leicester defenders, but looked slightly off balance at the crucial moment and ended up prodding the ball wide of Wallington's post. On a rare foray up field, Leicester did manage to force a corner that uncharacteristically Shilton dropped. Fortunately, O'Hare was on hand to clear the danger. For most of this match, the Foxes' main tactic had been to launch hopeful balls towards the head of Waddle; meat and drink for Forest's central defenders.

After a series of raids that produced numerous corners, Forest were awarded an eighty-ninth minute penalty; it just wasn't Leicester's day. Up stepped ace penalty taker John Robertson to smack the ball home. The ref blew, and that was that, two more points in the bag, thank you very much.

The table after the first seven League games:

	PLD	W	D	L	F	A	PTS
Man City	7	5	2	0	15	3	12
Forest	**7**	**6**	**0**	**1**	**15**	**6**	**12**
Liverpool	7	5	2	0	11	2	12
WBA	7	4	2	1	15	9	10

Sheffield United parted company with manager Jimmy Sirrel on 27 September.

Leicester City 0

Nottingham Forest 3
O'Neill (18), Woodcock (63),
Robertson (penalty 89)

Leicester City v. Nottingham Forest

John O'Hare in action.

Leicester City: Wallington, Whitworth, Rofe, Kember, Sims, Woollett, Robertson L., Sammels, Worthington, Waddle, Armstrong. Sub: Alderson

Nottingham Forest: Shilton, Anderson, Barrett, McGovern, Lloyd, Burns, O'Neill, Bowyer, O'Hare, Woodcock, Robertson. Sub: Haslegrave

Nottingham Forest v. Norwich City

Football League First Division, City Ground
Attendance: 23,741

Date: Saturday 1 October 1977
Referee: Mr M.R. Baker (Wolverhampton)

Forest's first draw of the season. This was a tight game, played on a horrible day, in which both defences looked to be well in control. An hour before the kick-off the fans had over an hour of torrential rain to contend with, then the sun came out.

Kenny Burns scored his first goal for Forest. Apart from that, the most important news was that Archie Gemmill was to make his League debut for Forest following his move from the Baseball Ground. The teams took the field in brilliant sunshine, Archie Gemmill leading out Forest; not only had he taken McGovern's place, but also the captaincy.

Forest started as normal. Ball out to Robertson, down the wing a bit, ball over, right to Woodcock's feet and on to big Pete, but this time unfortunately for Withe the ball was just out of his reach and ran harmlessly out of play. The crowd applauded Gemmill's first tackle, dumping Reeves on the ground and coming away with the ball. Norwich, following their usual policy of all-out attack at home or away, came back to force a corner, which failed to cause any problems for the Reds' defence. Then their forwards were caught offside on a couple of occasions, before Martin Peters got in a twenty-five-yard effort that Shilton caught cleanly.

The Canaries had set out their stall to limit Robbo's effectiveness, Ryan was detailed to sit in front of Kevin Bond and double-up on the winger. In doing so, when they could, the Norwich pair dished out an excessive amount of kicks and shoves on Robertson. However, most of the time Robbo managed to skip past their challenges to get in his cross, and on other occasions to win a free-kick. His next centre was flicked on by Woodcock, but again Withe was unable to reach the ball. From Bond's next animalistic infringement; a scything tackle on the Forest winger, Robbo squared a great ball to Burns, which the defender hit well, but unfortunately over the bar for a goal-kick.

Shots rained in on Keelan's goal from all angles, however none found the target. Norwich forced a couple of corners, and Peters brought a good save from Shilts with another speculative long-range effort. The rain came bucketing down again, adding miserably to the swirling wind that had been buffeting the players in the first half. No goals at the break was not a true reflection of the number of efforts on goal.

The good news was that Kenny Burns, who had taken a knock in the first period, was able to come out for the second half, but was clearly not at full throttle. Norwich capitalised on this and launched a number of purposeful raids and Shilton had to be alert to clear the danger. First, he leapt high to punch out a fierce shot from Gibbins, then bravely threw himself to his left to tip a shot from the same player around the post. An error by Kevin Keelan almost let in Forest when the 'keeper clumsily threw the ball straight to Robertson who wasted no time in crossing the ball to the onrushing Withe, but somehow the big striker contrived to scoop the ball high into the crowd. Soon

Nottingham Forest 1
Burns (73)

Norwich City 1
Peters (78)

Nottingham Forest v. Norwich City

after, the industrious Archie Gemmill failed by inches to meet Woodcock's low centre, then Bowyer almost scored with a diving header. Moments later, following good work by Gemmill, Peter Withe missed another sitter before the breakthrough finally came in the seventy-third minute. Robertson took a corner that screamed into the area, and Kenny Burns, racing in, met it flush to power a header past Keelan.

Norwich weren't about to lie down and stormed back, resulting in Barrett earning himself a booking for pulling back Jimmy Neighbour. Then Norwich grabbed a surprise equaliser. There seemed little danger as Sullivan's long clearance looped into the Forest penalty area until Shilton slipped, allowing England World Cup-winner Martin Peters to glance a header into the gaping goal to rescue a point for the Canaries. In the final moments of the game Forest might have nicked it, when Kenny Burns strode forward purposefully, but he skied his shot well over the bar.

The table after the first eight League games:

	PLD	W	D	L	F	A	PTS
Man City	8	5	3	0	16	4	13
Forest	**8**	**6**	**1**	**1**	**16**	**7**	**13**
WBA	8	5	2	1	17	10	12
Liverpool	8	5	2	1	11	4	12
Man Utd	8	4	2	2	11	7	10
Leeds	8	3	4	1	14	12	10

On 9 points were Everton, Arsenal, Wolves, Coventry, Norwich and Ipswich.

Also on 1 October 1977, the world's best and most famous player, Edson Arantes do Nascimento, better known to the entire world as Pelé, played his final game in the match between New York Cosmos and Santos of Brazil.

Tony Woodcock was selected for the England Under-21 squad to play Finland at Hull on 12 October.

A second team from East Anglia was next to visit Nottingham. Norwich may have got a point, but Forest weren't about to let Bobby Robson's Ipswich leave with anything.

Opposite: Kenny Burns.

Nottingham Forest: Shilton, Anderson, Barrett, Bowyer, Lloyd, Burns, O'Neill, Gemmill, Withe, Woodcock, Robertson. Sub: McGovern
Norwich City: Keelan, Bond K., Sullivan, Ryan, Jones, Powell, Neighbour, Reeves, Gibbins, Suggett, Peters. Sub: Lythgoe

Nottingham Forest v. Ipswich Town

Football League First Division, City Ground
Attendance: 26,845

Date: Tuesday 4 October 1977
Referee: Mr J.B. Worrall (Warrington)

Forest got back on track again with this superb victory over Bobby Robson's Ipswich. All four goals were scored by Peter Withe, as if to re-emphasise his claims for an England squad call-up from Ron Greenwood, who had so far failed to select him. Peter Shilton was the only Forest player in a squad of twenty-two for the World Cup qualifier in Luxembourg on 12 October. Ipswich had five in the squad – something was obviously wrong with that particular fact!

The second half of this game was beyond doubt 'The Peter Withe Show' as the Forest target man carved his name into the record books, alongside this sparkling exhibition of attacking football by the Reds. Forest ripped into one of England's most skilful sides with ninety minutes of aggressive running, topped with an abundance of fluent skills. For the best part of the first half Ipswich showed their defensive pedigree, playing a compact and well-organised brand of football designed to make life extremely difficult for any attackers. Unfortunately for them, on this October evening they found themselves up against one of the most potent attacks in the League, and the meanest defence imaginable.

The most severe of critics might suggest that this Forest rout occurred because Bobby Robson's side were having a real 'off' night. This was not the case. The inspired victory was conjured by Forest using all of the best footballing qualities. Four-nil it finished, but had it not been for Paul Cooper's defiant resistance, coupled with England defender Kevin Beattie's timely challenges, there can be no doubt that Forest would have run up a cricket score.

Having said that, the Ipswich 'keeper still found himself outclassed by a string of superb reflex saves from Peter Shilton, who at times was simply world class. Any England boss witnessing the dazzling stops he made to keep out efforts from Whymark and Mills must surely select him ahead of Ray Clemence, who seemed to be the current flavour of the month. Shilts saved the best till last, denying Beattie what looked a certain goal.

In front of Shilton, Larry Lloyd was also at his brilliant best, and along with Kenny Burns, the goalscoring double act of Paul Mariner and Trevor Whymark hardly got a sniff. But, in the end, this was Peter Withe's night; scoring four goals in a match is a tremendous feat. However I'm sure that Forest's number nine would be first to acknowledge the fantastic help he received from that doyen of the left wing, the irrepressible John Robertson, already a legend in English football. Ipswich held out for forty-three minutes until Withe got his first in the critical few minutes leading up to the break. Robbo took a quick throw-in, sending the ball to Withe who returned it to the Scottish winger. Withe headed for the box while Robbo teased his way up the wing, before curling a slide-rule cross for Withe to glance his header past Cooper. At half-time the board read 1-0 to Forest.

The second half saw Forest straight onto the attack determined to increase their lead. However it was a further thirteen minutes before the second goal came. This time Withe raced in to side-foot

Nottingham Forest 4   **Ipswich Town 0**
Withe 4 (43, 58, 86, 89)

Tony Woodcock.

the ball home from close range. The game ebbed and flowed for quite a while, Forest attacking, Ipswich defending, and then in the eighty-sixth minute, Robertson found his way past a couple of Ipswich defenders to whip in a low cross that Withe crashed into the net. Three minutes later, again from a Robertson cross, big Pete rapped home his and Forest's fourth with gusto.

Forest had simply sliced through a defence that previously had only conceded five goals in eight games. Although it was right that Withe captured the headlines, it would be wrong to forget the enormous contribution made by Tony Woodcock, who had one of those games when no matter what he did, he couldn't score. His unlucky efforts included a great shot that slammed against the bar, and one in the second half that brought a great save from Cooper. Withe slid the ball into his path and, after bringing it under control, he rifled in a near-perfect volley that the Ipswich goalie dived brilliantly to keep out. Cooper also denied Ian Bowyer's left-foot cracker that dipped wickedly towards the net before the former Blues 'keeper palmed the ball away. Martin O'Neill too found Cooper more than equal to a couple of stingers following some seriously powerful running. In the dying minutes, only an offside decision against another Forest player robbed Larry Lloyd of a goal that would have capped his fine display. His perfectly struck left-foot shot simply flew into the net, only for the ref to rule it out!

NOTTINGHAM FOREST V. IPSWICH TOWN

Despite managing to put a stranglehold on the early phase of this game, Ipswich were eventually forced to bend in the face of Forest's footballing extravaganza. Even a few dodgy refereeing decisions couldn't take anything away from Forest's outstanding performance, which built and built until exploding into four great goals. This emphatic win over a fancied team like Ipswich would certainly make a lot of people sit up and take notice of Nottingham Forest, who now knew that they could live with the very best.

The news that Manchester City had lost 4-2 at Coventry, Albion had lost 3-1 at Everton and that Liverpool had only managed a draw at Arsenal, meant that Forest went top, gaining a 2-point advantage on their nearest rivals at the top of the table.

The table after the first nine League games:

	PLD	W	D	L	F	A	PTS
Forest	**9**	**7**	**1**	**1**	**20**	**7**	**15**
Man City	9	5	3	1	18	8	13
Liverpool	9	5	3	1	11	4	13
WBA	9	5	2	2	18	13	12
Everton	9	4	3	2	16	9	11
Coventry	9	5	1	3	17	14	11
Arsenal	9	4	2	3	10	5	10

The latest breaking news in the city was that Ron Fenton had been sacked at Notts County and that Jimmy Sirrel was back as manager after two years as boss of Sheffield United.

On Friday evening, 7 October 1977, five people were injured by the 'Jet Machine' ride at the Goose Fair when floorboards surrounding the ride collapsed under the weight of spectators, tipping up to hit one of the spinning jets. Two children were treated in hospital and three other people received first aid.

Nottingham Forest: Shilton, Anderson, Barrett, McGovern, Lloyd, Burns, O'Neill, Bowyer, Withe, Woodcock, Robertson. Sub: O'Hare

Ipswich Town: Cooper, Burley, Tibbott, Talbot (Lambert), Hunter, Beattie, Mills, Gates, Mariner, Whymark, Woods.

WEST HAM UNITED v. NOTTINGHAM FOREST

Football League First Division, Upton Park
Attendance: 26,128

Date: Saturday 8 October 1977
Referee: Mr C.A. Maskell (Cambridgeshire)

As usual, Forest were away from home on 'Goose Fair Saturday'. After the previous result against West Ham, Forest fans could be excused for being disappointed that their boys didn't hammer the Hammers again. That five-goal drubbing provided a good lesson in how not to play against Forest; obviously the lads from 'the Smoke' were quick learners who weren't about to be caught napping again.

West Ham's players stuck to their allotted tasks, stifling every move Forest made to score an elusive goal, and generally raising their game. In fact, in the early portion of the game, of the two goalkeepers, it was Shilton that was called into action most frequently, pulling off saves from John Radford and Derek Hales. It was not until well into the first half that the League leaders troubled Mervyn Day. Peter Withe raced in, chasing Kenny Burns' free-kick, but the Hammers' goalkeeper beat him to the ball, punching well clear of the danger zone. A foul by Burns for obstructing Radford had almost disastrous results. Brooking rolled the ball to Tommy Taylor for the defender to rattle in a thunderbolt of a shot from fully twenty-five-yards out that had Shilton diving to keep the ball out.

Then it was West Ham's turn to give away a free-kick. Robertson swung in the ball, but Withe's header missed the target. Two minutes later, Shilton was out smartly, diving to his right to stop a fine effort by Radford. Pike crossed a great ball that Radford headed over the bar when maybe he should have at least worked the 'keeper. West Ham kept up a barrage of shots; Devonshire, Radford and Pike all going close, Brooking hitting Shilton with one effort.

At the other end, Robertson and O'Neill set up Bowyer, before Brooking and Curbishley did the same for Pike. Then a fine shot by Alan Curbishley forced Shilton to palm the ball over the bar. In one of the best moves of the game, Pike fed Brooking, but the England midfielder's cross came to nothing and the teams left the pitch at half-time with the score locked at 0-0.

Bowyer was forced to leave the field after taking a nasty knock to the head, and on came substitute Archie Gemmill. Under Radford's challenge, Barrett gave away a corner, which Shilton fisted clear. Suddenly it was end-to-end action all the way, with both sides coming close to breaking the deadlock. Pike whipped in a shot that almost caught Shilton out, the big 'keeper diving to palm the ball onto the foot of the post. Lloyd headed over, and then Radford looped a header over the bar, before toe-poking another effort just wide of the post In the dying stages of the game, Gemmill put through Barrett, but his first-time volley flew high and wide.

On the evening of 12 October, Tony Woodcock grabbed a hat-trick for England Under-21s as they murdered Finland 8-1 at Hull, making it four wins out of four to top their group. England's other scorers were: Deehan (2), Sims, Daniel (penalty) and Cunningham.

West Ham United 0   Nottingham Forest 0

West Ham United v. Nottingham Forest

Peter Shilton.

The full side played a World Cup qualifier in Luxembourg, beating them 2-0 with goals from Kennedy and Mariner. England: Clemence, Cherry, Hughes (Capt.), McDermott (Whymark), Watson (Beattie), Kennedy, Wilkins, Francis, Mariner, Hill, Callaghan. England really needed to score more goals than this; Italy had beaten the Luxembourgers 4-0 in their corresponding fixture.

Also that night, Scotland beat Wales 2-0 at Anfield to qualify for the 1978 World Cup finals in Argentina, and Northern Ireland, with Martin O'Neill on the right of midfield, were beaten 1-0 by Holland in Belfast to end their World Cup dream. Holland had booked their trip to Argentina.

A day later came the news that at long last the freedom-of-contract dispute was over. The Football League clubs had finally bowed to the inevitable and voted to accept the PFA's proposals. A spokesman said that details of the agreement would be released in due course.

West Ham United: Day, Lampard, Brush, Curbishley, Taylor T., McGiven, Devonshire, Robson B., Radford, Brooking, Pike. Sub: Taylor A.

Nottingham Forest: Shilton, Anderson, Barrett, McGovern, Lloyd, Burns, O'Neill, Bowyer (Gemmill), Withe, Woodcock, Robertson.

Nottingham Forest v. Manchester City

Football League First Division, City Ground
Attendance: 35,572

Date: Saturday 15 October 1977
Referee: Mr D.W. Lloyd (Worcestershire)

Still top of the table, Forest beat much-fancied Manchester City in a thrilling contest. Tony Book's Sky Blues were challenging neck-and-neck with the Reds at the top of the table, so something had to give. Manchester City deservedly took the lead in the twenty-first minute through Brian Kidd. A dangerous-looking corner was whipped over into the Reds' penalty area, Booth headed back towards goal, and there was ex-United starlet Brian Kidd to steer the ball home. Then a frustrated Kenny Burns hauled down Kidd and received a booking. Withe, who was obviously not happy with the situation, protested strongly, and was also booked. Brian Clough was not very pleased.

Robbo was brilliant, at times turning Paul Power inside out to set up numerous chances. Martin O'Neill was forced wide as he got in his shot, the ball ending up in the side netting. Kenny Burns leapt athletically to meet Robertson's left-wing corner, only to see his powerful header saved low to his right by Corrigan. It looked odds-on that City would go two up when a long clearance eventually reached Dennis Tueart, but just when most in the crowd thought he must score, somehow Barrett scrambled across to get in a timely challenge. In the thirty-fourth minute, another dazzling run by John Robertson produced the equaliser for the Reds. Robbo accelerated away leaving a trail of mesmerised City defenders in his wake. His cross eluded Corrigan to provide Woodcock with the easy task of running the ball into the net. Further incidents had both sets of fans in various stages of expectation and fear, but half-time came with neither side managing to grab a second goal.

In the first incident of the second period, Anderson fouled Power, and Barnes' free-kick cannoned off Lloyd for a corner, which thankfully produced nothing. The ball was quickly fed to the City end of the pitch, but O'Neill was easily dispossessed. Barnes, following up. fired in a shot that was well wide. Anderson again halted City's attack, this time hauling down Channon on the edge of the area as he shaped to shoot. The young full-back received a caution for his indiscretion. A couple of City forwards ran over the ball before Kidd sent the free-kick way off target. Channon was beginning to cause problems, and won a right-wing corner with a surging run. Barnes floated the ball over to Owen, whose rising shot missed the angle of post and bar by a few inches. Dennis Tueart was injured in the incident, and after treatment had to leave the field to be substituted by Clements.

A right-wing cross from O'Neill was neatly headed on by Woodcock to Withe but the centre forward struck his shot over the bar. Forest went close twice more in this period. First it looked a goal when O'Neill hammered in a right-foot cracker that Doyle bravely headed off the line with Corrigan well beaten, then Woodcock got in on the act with a fierce rising drive that Corrigan managed to get a hand to.

Archie Gemmill replaced Martin O'Neill, and nearly broke the deadlock, but his effort was blocked. Then with four minutes to go, the Scot combined with fellow countryman Robertson to set up Withe, whose shot deflected into the net off a City defender to wrap up the points for Forest; his

---

Nottingham Forest 2
Woodcock (34), Withe (86)

Manchester City 1
Kidd (21)

eleventh goal of the season. Even so, Cloughie fined him £50 for getting himself booked for dissent.

The table after the first eleven League games:

	PLD	W	D	L	F	A	PTS
Forest	**11**	**8**	**2**	**1**	**22**	**8**	**18**
Liverpool	11	7	3	1	15	5	17
Everton	11	6	3	2	22	10	15
Man City	11	6	3	2	21	11	15
WBA	11	6	3	2	20	14	15
Coventry	11	6	2	3	20	16	14

In another Monday night friendly, this one on 17 October, Forest walloped Second Division Sheffield United 6-1.

In a newspaper interview, it was reported that Derby's Tommy Docherty had called for Cloughie to be installed as England's new boss, but, he added, 'The powers that be won't hire Clough, they're too scared of him.' Cloughie was also in the press when he criticised those that he called 'The foul-mouthed fans at Forest.' He said that he was sick and tired of their behaviour: 'All they could do was chant abuse and obscenities at opposing players and fans instead of getting behind their team.'

Born in Nottingham on 29 August 1956, **Viv Anderson** joined Forest straight from school as an apprentice in November 1972, signing professional forms in August 1974. Viv made his senior debut at the age of eighteen, on 21 September 1974 against Sheffield Wednesday, his first of 430 first-team outings, including 5 as substitute, before transferring to Arsenal in August 1984 for £250,000, where he made 120 League appearances. He subsequently moved to Manchester United, playing 54 League games for Alex Ferguson, before moving to Sheffield Wednesday on a free transfer. Viv played in the Owls side that reached the FA Cup final in 1993, only to lose 2-1 to Arsenal in the replay after drawing 1-1 in the first game. He was a member of the Forest side that won the European Cup in 1979 and 1980. Highly rated full-back Viv Anderson was the first black player to represent England, making his international debut in the 1-0 win over Czechoslovakia at Wembley on 29 November 1978. He went on to win 30 full England caps, to add to his single Under-21 cap, between November 1978 and May 1988, scoring 2 goals for his country. He played for England in the 1980 European Championship Finals along ex-teammate Tony Woodcock. He also played 7 times for the England 'B' team. At the end of his playing career, Anderson had a short spell as manager of Barnsley, before becoming assistant manager to Bryan Robson at Middlesbrough.

Nottingham Forest: Shilton, Anderson, Barrett, McGovern, Lloyd, Burns, O'Neill (Gemmill), Bowyer, Withe, Woodcock, Robertson.

Manchester City: Corrigan, Power, Donachie, Owen, Doyle, Booth, Barnes, Channon, Kidd, Hartford, Tueart (Clements).

QUEENS PARK RANGERS v. NOTTINGHAM FOREST

Football League First Division, Loftus Road   **Date:** Saturday 22 October 1977
Attendance: 24,248   **Referee:** Mr M.J. Taylor (Deal)

Larry Lloyd captained the side in the absence of John McGovern, who would miss this game with a thigh strain, Archie Gemmill replacing him in midfield for this bruising, and at times scrappy affair that Rangers so desperately didn't want to lose, and Forest so richly deserved to win. Rangers frequently resorted to the offside trap as one of their main weapons of defence.

Soon after kick-off, Kenny Burns was in trouble after hauling down Peter Eastoe on the edge of the area. Don Givens made a near-post run to meet Masson's beautifully flighted free-kick, his smart header beating the diving Shilton to flash narrowly wide. Then Anderson upended Eastoe to give away another free-kick. The enigmatic Stan Bowles dummied to hit a shot but ran over the ball, allowing Don Masson to attempt to fool Shilton with a subtle chip, which went the wrong side of the post as far as QPR were concerned.

Tony Woodcock collected the ball in the QPR half and did well to hold off Clements and Shanks before feeding Withe, who in turn put in a neat ball to O'Neill, but the Irishman screwed wide of Parkes' goal. Then Archie Gemmill played the ball to Lloyd, whose fierce first-time effort was well saved by the ex-Walsall goalkeeper. Hollins cracked in another free-kick that ricocheted to safety off Anderson. Bowles and Masson had been impressive in Rangers' first-half performance; however, there is no doubt that Forest should have gone in at least one goal up instead of nil-all at the break.

The second forty-five minutes was to prove every bit as competitive as the first. Don Givens had been injured before the break, and Rangers brought on Williams. Straight away Bowles went close, his stinging shot flashing past the post. Forest renewed their efforts, O'Neill forcing a corner after some good work by Gemmill and Woodcock. Robertson sent in a swerving centre that Woodcock headed just off target and at the other end Shilton had to get down quickly to stop a shot from Gillard on his line. Just prior to the hour, all Rangers' hard work was undone by Ian Bowyer. Robbo raced along the left and whipped in a low cross, which Parkes only succeeded in diverting into the path of Forest's flame-haired midfielder, who dispatched the ball clinically into the net.

Back came the R's with a Don Masson left-wing corner that was eventually kicked off the line by Barrett after Shilton had stopped Hollins' shot. A string of scary situations followed, bringing Forest hearts into mouths. Williams, who was now getting into the game, severely tested Anderson with his running, getting in a number of dangerous crosses that Lloyd and Burns were relieved to head away. Then came the goal that sealed the points for the Reds.

On eighty-two minutes, Withe was fouled, and Kenny Burns curled in a stunning free-kick that flew past big Phil Parkes to wrap it up for Forest.

Queens Park Rangers 0   Nottingham Forest 2

Bowyer (59), Burns (82)

Queens Park Rangers v. Nottingham Forest

Tony Woodcock.

The table after the first twelve League games:

	PLD	W	D	L	F	A	PTS
Forest	**12**	**9**	**2**	**1**	**24**	**8**	**20**
Liverpool	12	7	4	1	15	5	18
WBA	12	7	3	2	24	14	17
Everton	12	6	4	2	22	10	16
Man City	12	6	3	3	21	13	15
Coventry	12	6	3	3	21	17	15
Norwich	12	6	3	3	14	16	15

This was a really nice position to be in as Forest took on their Nottingham neighbours in the third round of the Football League Cup.

Queens Park Rangers: Parkes, Clement, Gillard, Hollins, Needham, Shanks, Eastoe, Busby, Masson, Bowles, Givens (Williams).

Nottingham Forest: Shilton, Anderson, Barrett, Gemmill, Lloyd, Burns, O'Neill, Bowyer, Withe, Woodcock, Robertson. Sub: Birtles

Nottingham Forest v. Notts County

Football League Cup third round, City Ground
Attendance: 26,931

Date: Tuesday 25 October 1977
Referee: Mr A. Grey (Great Yarmouth)

Wow! What a performance gainst the Magpies. Nine goals in two games so far in this competition as Forest almost seemed to be scoring for fun. Having transferred England Under-21 goalkeeper John Middleton to Derby earlier in the season, Clough was forced to bring in the untried young 'keeper Chris Woods for his first outing of the season in place of cup-tied Shilton. Young England goalie Chris was still three weeks short of his eighteenth birthday. Archie Gemmill was also cup-tied, so John McGovern was recalled to the starting line-up. With both Les Bradd and Alan Birchenall still unfit, County manager Jimmy Sirrel kept the same team that had won their first League game of the season the Saturday before, beating Charlton 2-0.

The Magpies must have been quite pleased when the third-round draw paired them with their near-neighbours, such had been the success of their recent trips across the Trent. However, on this occasion, Second Division County were no match for slick Forest, as the Reds powered their way into the fourth round with two lovely goals from Ian Bowyer, plus one from Tony Woodcock, and a penalty from John Robertson that had started the proceedings.

Forest were first to show, with two half-chances for John McGovern, the second of which was the best, but the Reds' skipper snatched at the chance and pulled the ball well wide. Then after a couple of Notts raids had raised the temperature a little, Forest took the lead from the penalty spot. Just inside the County box, former Forest favourite Sammy Chapman took away Woodcock's legs for what was a clear penalty. Robbo placed a well-struck shot wide of Eric McManus' right hand as the 'keeper guessed the direction correctly. Soon after, a good run by Arthur Mann set up a great chance for Mick Vinter, but the striker, not realising how much time he had, blazed the ball over the crossbar. Notts stepped up their attacks, and John Sims got in a fierce shot that Colin Barrett managed to get a block on. Minutes later, Sims was again out of luck, this time being denied by debut boy Chris Woods. Half-time: 1-0 to Forest.

A minute after the restart, County's hopes were dashed by a second Forest goal. Exchanging passes with Peter Withe, Tony Woodcock fired the ball past McManus to give Notts a mountain to climb. Steve Carter was having no success against Barrett, and switched wings to see if he could fare any better against Viv Anderson, but the little winger got no change there either, eventually being booked for dissent in what was a frustrating afternoon for him. Sirrel took off Sims and sent on substitute Ian Scanlon to see if that would change their luck. Unfortunately for Nott,s shortly afterwards they were stunned by a killer third goal for the Reds.

On sixty-five minutes, Withe and Woodcock again combined well in a move that ended with McManus diving bravely at Woodcock's feet, who looked suspiciously offside. The loose ball was collected by Bowyer, who dispatched it into the net. County's defenders looked daggers at the linesman when he hadn't raised his flag, and it was 3-0 to Forest with twenty-five minutes left to

---

Nottingham Forest 4
Robertson (penalty 16),
Woodcock (46), Bowyer 2 (65, 84)

Notts County 0

NOTTINGHAM FOREST v. NOTTS COUNTY

Ian Bowyer.

play. Notts were understandably demoralised, and Forest took advantage with a fourth in the eighty-fourth minute. Peter Withe shielded the ball well, and turned it into the run of Ian Bowyer, who gleefully smacked it home. There was no way back for the brave Magpies, 4-0 emphasising the huge chasm in class between the two teams.

With the latest hurdle of the League Cup safely negotiated, Forest's next game would be against Cloughie's home town team.

Nottingham Forest: Woods, Anderson, Barrett, McGovern, Lloyd, Burns, O'Neill, Bowyer, Withe, Woodcock, Robertson. Sub: O'Hare

Notts County: McManus, Richards P., O'Brien, Chapman, Stubbs, Benjamin, Carter, Smith, Sims (Scanlon), Mann, Vinter.

NOTTINGHAM FOREST v. MIDDLESBROUGH

Football League First Division, City Ground   **Date:** Saturday 29 October 1977
Attendance: 27,373   **Referee:** Mr A.E. Morrissey (Bramhall)

Top-of-the-table Forest continued their October goal-fest with another four beauties; this time it was Boro's turn to be on the receiving end. One newspaper report that Irish winger Martin O'Neill had been relegated to the subs bench to make way for Archie Gemmill seemed a bit harsh. Boro made three changes: right full-back John Craggs returned after missing three games, one-time Wrexham centre forward Billy Ashcroft was fit again to lead the attack, and Ian Bailey moved from right-back to left-back in place of ex-Leeds and England star Terry Cooper who was still suffering from a knee injury.

Forest were determined to keep their unbeaten run going, and began the game in style. Viv Anderson put the Reds in front just after the half-hour mark by firing home spectacularly his first goal of the season. The young full-back then got another before the interval, after Ian Bowyer had scored Forest's second. As is evident from the scoreline, Middlesbrough's defensive strategy had backfired on them. Having said that, before Viv notched the opening goal, Boro had a spell when with a little bit of luck they might have taken the lead. Left-back Bailey's run took him past Anderson, and his cross found Graeme Souness on the edge of the goal area. Seeing the danger unfold, Shilton sprinted off his line to smother the ball at the midfielder's feet. Back came Forest through Bowyer, first with a snap shot after running through the Boro defence, and then leaping high to head over Barrett's centre. Platt had to be alert, leaving his line to fist away Robbo's cross before it reached Withe. Then it was Shilton's turn to impress, tipping McAndrew's header over for a corner after good work by Souness. Shilton was then pleased to punch the resultant corner out of harm's way.

Jim Platt was playing well, pushing away one effort, punching out another, and then conceding a corner from Withe's excellent drive. Woodcock and Barrett had shots blocked, and Platt held on to a rocket of a centre from Peter Withe. However, on thirty-one minutes the 'keeper was powerless to prevent Forest's first. Viv Anderson collected a loose ball in the Boro half, and when no challenge came, took it forward to the edge of the eighteen-yard line, before unleashing a tremendous right-foot cannonball that bulged the far corner of the Boro net, leaving Platt nonplussed.

In a moment of frustration, Ramage earned a booking for pulling down Woodcock, and from the free-kick Woodcock squared to Burns, whose right-foot shot skimmed the upright. Then McGovern did the same. Five minutes before the break, Robertson waltzed past Souness and Craggs, before floating in an inviting centre that Bowyer accepted gleefully to head powerfully past Platt. Then it was the Anderson show again. Almost on the stroke of half-time, the impressive full-back latched onto Burns' clearance, and in a repeat of his earlier effort, made directly for goal, before crashing a left-foot shot beyond the Boro 'keeper. Three-nil at the interval.

Forest began the second half searching for a fourth goal, but their early efforts were kept out by Platt. The Boro goalkeeper made a huge slip-up in the fifty-fifth minute, when he carelessly allowed John McGovern's fierce right-foot shot to pass through his hands into the net. Boro went down to

---

Nottingham Forest 4   **Middlesbrough 0**
  Anderson 2 (31, 44),
  Bowyer (40), McGovern (55)

ten men when Ashcroft had to leave the field following a heavy challenge. He returned after several minutes of treatment, but was eventually replaced by substitute Hickton. Forest's fourth goal had given Boro a mountain to climb; a truly hopeless task, which obviously took its toll on their spirit as the Reds ended the game with a barrage of attempts on goal, which Platt heroically kept out. The names of Gemmill and McAndrew found their way into the referee's notebook for a 'handbags at ten yards' type of incident.

Kenny Burns was booked for dissent and fined by Clough, despite being adamant that he had said nothing to referee Tony Morrissey. Clough said later that he would await the referee's report, and that Burns would get his fine back if the ref proved his innocence.

The table after the first thirteen League games:

	PLD	W	D	L	F	A	PTS
Forest	**13**	**10**	**2**	**1**	**28**	**8**	**22**
Liverpool	13	7	4	2	16	8	18
Everton	13	6	5	2	26	14	17
Man City	13	7	3	3	24	14	17
WBA	13	7	3	3	25	16	17
Coventry	13	7	3	3	24	18	17

The Middlesbrough game had produced another fabulous victory for Forest. Now for the Chelsea pensioners.

Forest had a young striker on the fringes of the first-team, a player who was to become a huge star for the Reds. His name: **Garry Birtles**. Having made his first-team debut in the Division 2 game against Hull City at the City Ground on 12 March 1977, Garry Birtles was restricted to playing a support role in Forest's Championship winning season. His only involvement being as non-used substitute in the game at QPR on 22 October 1977. He had played in two of the pre-season tour games, scoring one in the 5-1 destruction of SV Plattling, plus an appearance in the 5-1 win against Neuburg in Germany, and made one further appearance in the friendly against Hartlepool United in November 1977. Garry was born in Nottingham on 27 July 1956, and arrived on the professional football scene like a meteor. After spells with Long Eaton Rovers and non-league Long Eaton FC, he was transferred to Nottingham Forest in March 1977 for a reported fee of £30,000. Establishing himself in the first-team in season 1978/79 following the departure of Peter Withe to Newcastle United, Garry banged in 26 goals in all competitions; 14 in the League, plus 6 in the League Cup including two in the winning Final against Southampton, a game in which he also had two others disallowed; and of course 6 in the European Cup as he helped Forest to the crown of European Champions. A feat that the Reds repeated in the following season.

Opposite: John McGovern.

Nottingham Forest: Shilton, Anderson, Barrett, McGovern, Lloyd (O'Neill) Burns, Gemmill, Bowyer, Withe, Woodcock, Robertson.
Middlesbrough: Platt, Craggs, Bailey, Souness, Boam, Ramage, Mahoney, Mills, Ashcroft (Hickton), McAndrew, Armstrong.

CHELSEA v. NOTTINGHAM FOREST

Football League First Division, Stamford Bridge   **Date:** Saturday 5 November 1977
Attendance: 36,116   **Referee:** Mr B. Stevens (Stonehouse)

Oh dear! What was it about the capital that Forest disliked? Not winning there too often, that's what. This time, it was the Blues' young nineteen-year-old striker Trevor Aylott that did the damage with his second goal in as many games.

Forest started confidently enough, as you would expect from a side leading the League. Robertson forced a corner on the left, which Larry Lloyd headed down to Bowyer, who from a narrow angle whipped in a ferocious shot that the diving Peter Bonetti managed to claw away. At the other end, Shilton had to get down smartly to keep out Aylott's first-timer from a Ray 'Butch' Wilkins pass. With Bonetti and Shilton vying for the best save of the day award, it was a toss-up as to which side would score first, if at all.

Using their mobility, Withe and Woodcock might have expected to do better against Chelsea's two giant central defenders, particularly Micky Droy, but each time the Forest strikers received the ball, Droy and Wicks were on hand to crowd them out. Bonetti pulled a couple more saves out of his top draw, and Bowyer went close with a right-foot blaster that looked certain to find the far corner. Somehow, Bonetti sprang to his right, stretched out an arm, and pushed the ball wide of the post. Then moments later, a Gemmill shot squirmed well wide. Bowyer pulled down Charlie Cooke which resulted in Viv Anderson having his name taken for dissent, a Clough fine no doubt on the way. The referee made Wilkins retake the free-kick, as he wasn't ready the first time, then blew his whistle for half-time, with the score at 0-0.

After the break, Chelsea attacked down the left, and Shilton had to be quick to gather a shot from Sparrow. The home side continued to press the visitors, and in the fifty-fifth minute grabbed the all-important first goal. Kenny Swain put Aylott away, and the young striker rifled a great shot past Shilton. Shilts' agility was severely tested in the next fifteen minutes, but the Forest 'keeper showed why he was the best in the business by stopping everything that Chelsea threw at him.

Peter Bonetti caused a few heart murmurs among the Chelsea fans when he dropped the ball with Lloyd pressing. Woodcock swung his boot, but his effort was blocked. Chelsea came away with the ball to create an incisive move that produced a fine shot which Shilton palmed away to Aylott, who fortunately thundered the loose ball wide of the post.

O'Neill replaced Bowyer as Forest searched for the equaliser, and almost got it when Withe and Gemmill went close. Burns headed over, Withe's screamer was blocked, and O'Neill fired past the post as Forest just couldn't find the killer punch. In the dying minutes, Shilton kept the score down to 1-0 with a fantastic save from young Trevor Aylott.

This was Forest's first defeat in ten games. Still, it wasn't enough to knock them off the top of the table.

Chelsea 1   **Nottingham Forest 0**
   Aylott (55)

Viv Anderson is challenged by Chelsea's Ray Lewington.

The table after the first fourteen League games:

	PLD	W	D	L	F	A	PTS
Forest	**14**	**10**	**2**	**2**	**28**	**9**	**22**
Everton	14	7	5	2	27	14	20
WBA	14	8	3	3	27	16	19
Coventry	14	8	3	3	25	18	19
Liverpool	14	7	4	3	17	10	18
Man City	14	7	3	4	24	15	17

Next up, those Red Devils from Manchester.

Chelsea: Bonetti, Wilkins G., Sparrow, Britton, Droy, Wicks, Aylott, Wilkins R., Langley, Swain, Cooke. Sub: Lewington

Nottingham Forest: Shilton, Anderson, Barrett, McGovern, Lloyd, Burns, Gemmill, Bowyer (O'Neill), Withe, Woodcock, Robertson.

Nottingham Forest v. Manchester United

Football League First Division, City Ground
Attendance: 30,183

Date: Saturday 12 November 1977
Referee: Mr G. Courtney (Spennymoor)

The Reds beat the Red Devils to retain their place at the top of the table, but not before a fifth minute scare when United went ahead through Stuart Pearson. The rain bucketed down, monsoon style, made worse by a vortex-like wind of high Beaufort scale proportions.

Forest literally slid into the attack from the off, with recalled Brian Greenhoff called into early service to prevent first Robertson and then Withe from getting in an attempt on goal. Greenhoff's third sliding tackle cost him a free-kick when the referee adjudged that he had caught Withe as he took the ball. Kenny Burns met Robbo's kick firmly, but Roche punched away his shot, and gathered the ball after Burns' follow-up ran across the six-yard box.

In United's first real attack, McGrath got the ball wide to McIlroy, whose cross on the run was headed past Shilton just inside the far post by Pearson; it was a bitter blow, five minutes gone and one down. Woodcock was looking bright, and had almost put the Reds ahead, but with only Roche to beat, placed his shot too close to the 'keeper who saved comfortably. The United defence had stopped, expecting the referee to blow for offside against Woodcock, which just shows you should always play to the whistle! The offside trap was a particular favourite tactic with the lads from Old Trafford, and they certainly weren't discouraged by this incident. In the first half they regularly caught Withe and Woodcock with this ploy.

United might have increased their lead through Pearson, who looked dangerous each time he got the ball. On his next foraging run, Shilton was helpless as he watched the striker's shot pass the outside of his post. Phew! Pearson went close again, but watched in disappointment as his rising drive cleared the angle of bar and post. Fortunately he was given offside as he received a pass from Coppell, and then the striker shot well wide. Just before the break, Gordon Hills crashed in a low shot that rebounded off Kenny Burns, who needed treatment to his injured knee before being able to continue. United had just about edged the first forty-five minutes, and were well worth their one-goal lead.

The second period began amid driving rain, with Forest's minds set on an early equaliser. Four minutes into the half, it came. Martin Buchan fouled Peter Withe twenty-five yards from goal, an obvious free-kick, from which McGovern slipped a quick pass to Gemmill, whose snap-shot bounced out to Burns. The Scot cracked the ball home to send the Forest fans wild with jubilation. United's defenders claimed offside, but referee George Courtney waved away their protests. Burns' goal fired up Forest to even greater endeavours. Woodcock was penalised after Gemmill had cleverly put him through. In the next twenty minutes, Shilton and Roche were kept busy as both sides went for the winner. Then with sixteen minutes to go, following a move of breathtaking proportions, Forest got the decisive breakthrough.

John McGovern won the ball in midfield, sending Robertson away in classic Forest style. Robertson found Withe, who carried the ball into the box before finding the head of the onrushing

Nottingham Forest 2
Burns (49), Gemmill (74)

Manchester United 1
Pearson (5)

Kenny Burns.

Archie Gemmill, who rounded off a move of the finest quality. Then the unthinkable happened. Woodcock was shaping to shoot, when Greenhoff took his legs from under him. Penalty! Yes, the ref pointed to the spot. Robbo placed the ball on the spot, paced out his run, and struck a firm shot that everyone except Roche thought would go in. The lanky Irish 'keeper, guessing Robbo's intention correctly, dived to his right to palm the ball away. A fabulous chance to finish off United was wasted.

Forest renewed their efforts to get the elusive third goal, leaving gaps at the back, which McGrath and McCreery almost exploited. Fortunately, Shilton was equal to everything they and their colleagues threw at him. No doubt the Forest fans were pleased to hear the whistle.

Nottingham Forest v. Manchester United

The table after the first fifteen League games:

	PLD	W	D	L	F	A	PTS
Forest	**15**	**11**	**2**	**2**	**30**	**10**	**24**
Everton	15	8	5	2	29	15	21
WBA	15	8	4	3	30	19	20
Coventry	15	8	4	3	26	19	20
Arsenal	15	7	4	4	18	10	18
Liverpool	15	7	4	4	17	12	18

Monday 14 November was the date of the next friendly, this one away to Hartlepool United. It was another draw, this one 2-2.

England played another World Cup qualifier on 16 November 1977, a 2-0 victory over Italy at Wembley with goals from Keegan and Brooking, to gain revenge for the 2-0 defeat by Italy in Rome on 17 November 1976. England: Clemence, Neal, Cherry, Wilkins, Watson, Hughes (Capt.), Keegan (Francis), Coppell, Latchford (Pearson), Brooking, Barnes. England, having completed their programme of matches, now headed the qualification table with 10 points from 6 games; goals for 15, goals against 4. The problem was that Italy, with 8 points and the exact same goals for and against as England, had one game left to play; on 3 December 1977, against Luxembourg. Only a miracle would see England qualify for the 1978 finals in Argentina.

Meanwhile, Forest were off to Yorkshire.

Born in Liverpool on 30 August 1951, **Peter Withe** had made a few appearances for Southport, Preston North End and Barrow, before trying his luck in South Africa with Port Elizabeth & Arcadia Shepherds, which was where he was spotted and recommended to Wolves, whom he joined, first on loan in September 1973, before being signed for £13,500 a month later. After making his Wanderers' debut in March 1974, he played for the Molineux outfit only another 14 times, plus 3 times as substitute over 2 seasons, scoring 3 goals, before moving to Portland Timbers in the NASL. He joined Birmingham City from Wolves, who still held his registration, for £50,000 in August 1975. That's where Brian Clough, not a bad judge of centre forwards, saw him and decided he would do a good job for Forest; bringing him to the City Ground in September 1976 for a fee of £42,000. Withe would never have claimed to be the most skilful striker around, but his qualities of bravery and hard work more than made up for what he lacked in skill. Clough eventually sold him to Newcastle United for £200,000 in September 1978, certainly a good profit. But after only 75 League appearances, including 1 as substitute, and 28 League goals, was the 'Old Master' too quick to cash in on his centre forward?

Nottingham Forest: Shilton, Anderson, Barrett, McGovern, Lloyd, Burns, Gemmill, Bowyer, Withe, Woodcock, Robertson. Sub: O'Neill

Manchester Utd: Roche, Nicholl, Houston, McIlroy, Greenhoff B., Buchan, McGrath, Coppell, Pearson, McCreery, Hill. Sub: Albiston

LEEDS UNITED v. NOTTINGHAM FOREST

Football League First Division, Elland Road
Attendance: 42,925

Date: Saturday 19 November 1977
Referee: Mr C.N. Seel (Carlisle)

United were no doubt pleased to put one over on former short-term manager Cloughie, in a game that Forest probably expected to win; the home fans certainly weren't making him feel welcome. Leeds were now without many of their old stars and were certainly nothing like the team that had won the League Championship in 1973/74. They had £100,000 summer signing from Aberdeen Arthur Graham on the left wing. Striker Ray Hankin passed a late fitness test to resume his partnership with the fiery Joe Jordan. This was a great pity, because it was Hankin that scored the only goal of the game to win it for Leeds.

The contest began as a bit of a chess game with both sides looking strong and full of purposeful running. Peter Withe had the best chance of the opening exchanges, heading narrowly wide of the target. Predictably, the home fans jeered John McGovern at every opportunity, none more so than when he blazed his shot way over from a good position. Frankie Gray had earlier seen his effort pass wide of Shilton's near post following an excellent run down the left. Moreover, shortly after, Jordan blatantly barged Lloyd out of his way before racing away. Fortunately, the fearsome-looking Scot screwed his shot well wide. Referee Seel and his linesman were probably the only people in the ground that did not see what had happened. Lloyd and Burns rounded upon the official, no doubt pointing out his error, in a genteel manner of course.

Archie Gemmill was in the thick of the action, tackling hard, chasing and harrying, and passing the ball around quite beautifully. One great pass set up Woodcock, but the young striker's right-foot drive cleared the angle. In the next ten minutes both sides went near to scoring, and then Forest scored what looked to be a perfectly good goal. On the half-hour mark, Woodcock deftly flicked Robbo's fine cross on to Withe, for the big centre forward to notch his first League goal since 15 October. However, the celebrations were short-lived as the referee reacted to his linesman's raised flag, signalling that the Forest player was in an offside position when he received the ball. Rats!

Leeds, spurred on by this fortuitous decision, attacked with more venom. Hankin brought a fabulous diving save from Shilton. Then the 'keeper took a nasty blow to his face, and although he was able to continue after treatment, he did not look right. Immediately, Graham sent a grubhunter across the Forest area, which Hankin controlled superbly before dispatching a low shot past the helpless Shilton. Big Pete needed more treatment before the game could restart. Would he have kept Leeds out if he had not been hurt? We will never know.

Half-time came and went; still Forest could not find the decisive breakthrough. Harvey had to be quick off his line to fist away a Burns free-kick, then Woodcock blazed over, Cherry challenging the young striker as he was about to pull the trigger. At the other end, Shilton palmed over Graham's swerving shot, and Hankin headed Harris's cross over the bar. Robbo bent in a shot, which unfortunately curled past Harvey's far post, and then the Leeds goalie athletically kept out

---

Leeds United 1
Hankin (36)

Nottingham Forest 0

Leeds United v. Nottingham Forest

goal-bound shots from Burns and Bowyer. In the final minutes, Frank Clark prevented what looked like a certain second for Leeds, when he raced back to clear off the line with Shilton beaten.

This was the last league match that Forest would lose in the entire season.

Fortunately, Everton, Liverpool and Albion could only manage to draw their games. Coventry and Arsenal won theirs.

The table after the first sixteen League games:

	PLD	W	D	L	F	A	PTS
Forest	**16**	**11**	**2**	**3**	**30**	**11**	**24**
Everton	16	8	6	2	32	18	22
Coventry	16	9	4	3	30	20	22
WBA	16	8	5	3	30	19	21
Arsenal	16	8	4	4	20	11	20
Liverpool	16	7	5	4	22	13	19

Down at the foot of the table, Newcastle were struggling with only 6 points. Last but one were Leicester with 9 points, a point ahead of West Ham.

A squad of fourteen Forest players, plus Cloughie, travelled to Israel for a quick three-day break in the sun, including a sightseeing trip to Jerusalem, and on Tuesday 22 November beat Maccabi Tel Aviv 6-1 in a friendly. They arrived back in the UK on Wednesday.

Also on Tuesday 22 November, Forest's rivals Liverpool travelled to Germany to play Kevin Keegan's Hamburg in the first leg of the Super Cup, David Fairclough scored their equaliser in a 1-1 draw.

Mr Versatile, **Ian Bowyer** was born in Ellesmere Port on 6 June 1951, birthplace of two other footballing giants, Stan Cullis and Joe Mercer. Bowyer had originally made his name at Manchester City, but ended up at Leyton Orient, when Dave Mackay brought him for Forest in October 1973. He went on to make a total of 541 appearances, plus 23 as substitute, (the second all-time highest number of appearances for Nottingham Forest), in two spells with the club, scoring many vital goals among his very respectable total of 96, (joint-seventh alongside Garry Birtles in Forest's top ten all-time goalscorers). He was sold to Sunderland in January 1981. Then Clough bought him back in January 1982, before eventually releasing him in May 1987. He is now on Forest's coaching staff.

Leeds United: Harvey, Cherry, Gray F., Currie, Parkinson, Madeley, Harris, Hankin, Jordan, Flynn, Graham. Sub: Gray E.

Nottingham Forest: Shilton, Anderson, Barrett, McGovern, Lloyd, Burns, Gemmill, Bowyer, Withe, Woodcock, Robertson. Sub: O'Hare.

John McGovern.

Nottingham Forest v. West Bromwich Albion

Football League First Division, City Ground
Attendance: 31,908

Date: Saturday 26 November 1977
Referee: Mr P.G. Reeves (Leicester)

Free-scoring West Bromwich Albion had finished the previous season in seventh place in the League. Under the stewardship of Johnny Giles they had become an attractive side, capable of beating anyone on their day. However, Giles had had enough and left at the end of the previous season. The Baggies had turned to Albion legend Ronnie Allen, who had signed a young man who was himself to become a Hawthorns' legend, Cyrille Regis, for the bargain price of £5,000. A clean sheet for suntanned Forest was welcome, but the worrying thing was that all of a sudden they couldn't score at the other end.

In a pulsating game, fourth-placed Albion held the division's pacesetters, largely due to a resolute defensive performance that dealt with everything that the Reds threw at them. In goal, the agile Tony Godden made two quite breathtaking saves from Gemmill and Woodcock.

This was a game in which two of the finest left-wing talents in the League were on display. For Albion, Willie Johnson, and of course Robbo for the Reds. Both were hoping to be called into the Scottish World Cup squad for 1978's tournament in Argentina.

In the early stages of the game, it was Robbo who provided the best chances, the pick of which were for McGovern, who fired wide, and Barrett, who headed inches past the post. Albion were another team to favour the frustrating offside tactic away from home, and managed to catch the Forest forwards time and time again. Peter Withe was looking decidedly out of sorts, the fact that he hadn't scored for six games was obviously playing heavy on his mind. When they did venture forward, the Baggies looked dangerous; obviously their goals scored total was no mirage. Laurie Cunningham and Tony Brown linked well on a number of occasions, often playing the ball into the powerful thrusting runs of Bryan Robson, and with Johnson sending over a stream of crosses it seemed that Forest would need to score at least a couple to beat their visitors.

Albion came forward again, and Shilton was stranded when Martin's deflected shot squirmed towards the line, fortunately, Robbo managed to touch the ball past the upright for a corner, which came to nothing. Nil-nil at the interval was probably a surprise to every one of the 30,000-plus crowd. Shilton was soon in action after the break, and then set up a move that ended when 'Bomber' Brown pulled down John McGovern to earn a booking from the referee. Woodcock went close, before Forest won a corner when McGovern's drive deflected off John Wile. Woodcock curled in the ball too near to Albion 'keeper Tony Godden who stretched his hands to gather, but somehow allowed the ball to slip from his grasp. A load of boots were swung, but sadly, it was one belonging to a Baggies' player that got there first. A second corner was comfortably cleared by Martin.

Opposite: Peter Withe.

Nottingham Forest 0   West Bromwich Albion 0

Nottingham Forest v. West Bromwich Albion

The play swung from end to end, with many thrilling situations served up for the supporters, however, neither side could create a clear-cut, gold-plated goalscoring opportunity. Near the end, the visitors had a couple of half-chances, and might have stolen the game from under Forest's noses. For Forest, that would have been a tragic injustice; they deserved at least a point. Then at the death, Gemmill and Johnson clashed in a nasty incident, and had to be lectured by the ref. Thankfully, the two fiery Scotsmen eventually calmed down, and the game ended in equanimity.

All week long, Clough had championed Baggies boss Ronnie Allen, saying that it was a disgrace that he had no contract. Albion's chairman Bert (later to be called 'Bert the Inert') Millichip, a member of England's management committee, told Cloughie to mind his own business – Cloughie never did get the England job, did he?

The top of the League table after seventeen games:

	PLD	W	D	L	F	A	PTS
Forest	**17**	**11**	**3**	**3**	**30**	**11**	**25**
Everton	17	9	6	2	38	18	24
WBA	17	8	6	3	30	19	22
Coventry	17	9	4	4	30	26	22
Liverpool	17	8	5	4	22	13	21
Man City	17	8	4	5	32	20	20

Fulham manager Bobby Campbell announced that he had suspended errant superstar George Best, who had apparently 'gone missing' again.

Next up was a midweek diversion as Forest entertained the holders in the fourth round of the Football League Cup, in the happy knowledge that they had already beaten them 2-0 in the League in September.

Nottingham Forest: Shilton, Anderson, Barrett, McGovern, Lloyd, Burns, O'Neill, Gemmill, Withe, Woodcock, Robertson. Sub: Bowyer
West Bromwich Albion: Godden, Mulligan, Statham, Tony Brown, Wile, Robertson, Martin, Cunningham, Cross, Robson, Johnston. Sub: Regis

Nottingham Forest v. Aston Villa

Football League Cup fourth round, City Ground **Date:** Tuesday 29 November 1977
Attendance: 29,333   **Referee:** Mr C. Thomas (Treorchy)

On this freezing cold November night, another four-goal performance saw Forest come out on top at the City Ground. Chris Woods got another game in goal for Forest in place of the cup-tied Peter Shilton. The Reds adapted to the icy conditions much better than Ron Saunders' boys from Brum.

Forest opened up powerfully and scored three goals in the first twenty-five minutes, as they completely outplayed Villa, hustling the visitors in typical fashion. First, it was Larry Lloyd who got in on the goalscoring act with his first goal of the season. The game was only seven minutes old when, under pressure from Peter Withe, Ken McNaught put the ball behind for a corner. Robbo's kick found the incoming Larry Lloyd at the near post, who glanced a twisting header past Rimmer.

Robertson skinned full-back Gidman to provide the killer ball to the far post for Viv Anderson, foraging upfield in his customary fashion, to put the Reds two up with a bullet header. Forest's third came in the twenty-fifth minute. John Robertson's corner was booted out of defence, but only as far as John McGovern, who rifled the ball at goal, where back-to-form Peter Withe got a foot to the fierce shot to deflect the ball past Jimmy Rimmer. Just before the break, the Villa goalkeeper produced a world-class save to keep out a wicked shot from John McGovern.

Three-nil at half-time was a true representation of the first forty-five minutes, with Robbo orchestrating much of the breathtaking football that Forest had played thus far. Along with Woodcock and Withe, the way the Scottish winger tore Villa apart was marvellous to witness. Seven minutes after the break, a terrible mistake by Ken McNaught cost Villa dear. The stylish number five attempted a forty-yard back-pass that got nowhere near Jimmy Rimmer, allowing Tony Woodcock to intercept the ball, take it round Rimmer, and slot it home for number four. Two minutes later Forest had a fifth goal disallowed when the hardworking Bowyer was judged to have been in an offside position before he had smacked the ball into the net.

Now it was all Forest. Colin Barrett exchanged passes with Peter Withe to create a great chance for Robertson, and he really should have scored. Then Robbo crossed to make another opening that this time Martin O'Neill met cleanly, only to see it saved on the line. For over an hour the Reds had Villa firmly on the rack, pulling their defenders every which way in a barnstorming display. Now understandably, Forest began to ease up, allowing Villa to come back into the game, and it's fair to say that they looked a lot better in the final twenty minutes of the game. In the sixty-sixth minute, Andy Gray crashed in a rising shot that hit the woodwork, but substitute Cowans couldn't make anything out of the rebound. On seventy-nine minutes, Ken McNaught headed down a Gordon Smith cross that Brian Little met perfectly to superbly smash in a great volley that flew into the top corner of the net. It was probably the best candidate for 'goal of the game.' Then five minutes before the end, Shilton's young deputy, Chris Woods let a fierce but harmless-looking Frank Carrodus cross-cum-shot slip through his hands for Villa's second.

Nottingham Forest 4
Lloyd (7), Anderson (13),
Withe (25), Woodcock (52)

Aston Villa 2
Little (79), Carrodus (85)

Nottingham Forest v. Aston Villa

Larry Lloyd.

In the closing minutes, Martin O'Neill blasted a good chance wide, before John McGovern drew a wonderful diving save from Rimmer who literally flew across the face of goal to acrobatically keep out the Forest skipper's goal-bound effort. Fortunately for Forest, Villa's recovery was a case of too little, too late, and the game ended 4-2 to the home side, giving the scoreline a decidedly false look. Both Ron Saunders and his captain Leighton Phillips blamed the icy conditions for their first defeat in thirteen League and cup games. A case of sour grapes surely; both teams were playing on the same surface! Now for the fifth round – the quarter-finals.

The newspapers reported 'a bit of a do' at the subsequent press conference. Apparently Cloughie told the assembled reporters 'I want nothing to do with the ******* press. I have finished with the *******. They are a shower and they stink in my opinion.' He walked out, only to return to say 'In case you did not hear correctly, then I'll repeat it.' And he did, word for word. Apparently, he was upset at the style and manner of reporting following the game with West Brom. The reporters saw some irony in the great man's choice of expletives. Earlier in the season, the press had reported that Clough had told-off Forest fans for swearing, and had installed a notice at the City Ground with the request, 'Gentlemen, please, no swearing.' He is still 'Superboss', nothing can ever change that.

The draw for the quarter-finals of the Football League Cup would see Forest take on Bob Stokoe's Bury at Gigg Lane.

At the draw for the 1978–80 European Championships, England were pitched against Denmark, Bulgaria, the Republic of Ireland, and Northern Ireland.

As for Forest, they were back on track goals-wise, and through to the fifth round of the League Cup. Best of all they were still top of the League. Off to Brum next.

Nottingham Forest: Woods, Anderson, Barrett, McGovern, Lloyd, Burns, O'Neill, Bowyer, Withe, Woodcock, Robertson. Sub: O'Hare

Aston Villa: Rimmer, Gidman, Smith, Phillips, McNaught, Mortimer, Deehan (Cowans), Little, Gray, Cropley, Carrodus.

BIRMINGHAM CITY v. NOTTINGHAM FOREST

Football League First Division, St Andrew's
Attendance: 29,925

Date: Saturday 3 December 1977
Referee: Mr B.H. Daniels (Brentwood)

This was Birmingham City old boys Kenny Burns and Peter Withe's first return to their old stamping ground St Andrew's, and a very pleasurable visit it turned out to be. Kenny kept wonder-boy Trevor Francis pretty quiet, apart from one chance a few minutes before half-time, which Shilton saved magnificently, the future Forest European Cup-winner hardly had a kick all afternoon. The Blues had spent a bit of money: £120,000 to Ipswich for Keith Bertschin and £140,000 to Man City for Tony Towers.

After the disappointment of the two previous League games, Forest began in determined fashion. Almost straight from the kick-off, the ball was played out to Robertson, who beat Calderwood before neatly playing in Woodcock. The young striker's cross was floated over, but to the cheers and jeers of the home fans, Withe put his header wide. The Blues looked competent in midfield, but weren't able to get past Lloyd and Burns, who also came in for a good deal of stick from the Brummies. Then Martin O'Neill put Forest one up after ten minutes, although there was an element of good fortune involved. Robbo flighted a left-wing corner, which reached McGovern, who rifled in a shot that O'Neill diverted past the helpless Montgomery. Then O'Neill won Forest another corner following a mazy run that took him past the Birmingham defence.

Bruising would not be an accurate description of the game at this point, but the flow was constantly interrupted by far too many free-kicks being awarded; a bit too much whistle! A good example of the referee's over-enthusiasm was when Kenny Burns beat Keith Bertschin in an aerial tussle that looked fair and equitable, for which the man in black gave Brum a free-kick: crazy! With the half coming to a close, the Blues forced a couple of corners, neither of which troubled the Forest defence. Then Shilton denied Bertschin an certain equaliser with a top-class save.

With Birmingham coming into the game a little more, Forest needed to force the pace and find another goal. This they did with their second attack of the second half. The architects of the move that preceded the goal were Gemmill and Robertson, who combined to put Withe clear on goal. Jim Montgomery raced off his line to dive bravely at the striker's feet, the ball cannoning off him for a corner. Woodcock slung over a great centre to the unmarked Larry Lloyd, whose downward header was booted off the goal line by Calderwood. The defender's clearance went straight to a Forest player, who was brought down. Anderson's fifty-second-minute swerving free-kick dropped dangerously into Birmingham's box, and after challenges from Withe and Burns, the ball rebounded fortuitously for Tony Woodcock to slot past Jimmy Montgomery with his right foot.

Just before the hour mark, Calderwood fired over the bar. Then substitute Tony Towers came on for Malcolm Page in the sixty-second minute. Forest were looking likely to extend their lead, and in their next attack, Jim Montgomery jumped courageously to fist away Robertson's vicious inswinging cross. A booking for Burns for bringing down Francis, a yard from the penalty area, brought an even

Birmingham City 0

Nottingham Forest 2
O'Neill (10), Woodcock (52)

BIRMINGHAM CITY v. NOTTINGHAM FOREST

Trevor Francis of Birmingham and England.

greater crescendo of jeers from Blues fans. Francis took the free-kick himself, blasting the ball into the red-shirted wall, and the danger was cleared. From then on, Forest took charge, taking the sting out of the game, worthy winners at 2-0.

The top of the League table after eighteen games:

	PLD	W	D	L	F	A	PTS
Forest	**18**	**12**	**3**	**3**	**32**	**11**	**27**
Everton	18	10	6	2	39	18	26
WBA	18	8	7	3	30	19	23
Liverpool	18	9	5	4	24	13	23
Coventry	18	9	5	4	31	27	23
Arsenal	18	9	4	5	22	14	22

Brian Clough was interviewed for the England job on 4 December 1977. An already-done deal was the phrase that sprang to many a pair of lips.

On 6 December Liverpool hosted the second leg of their 'Super Cup' match with Hamburg at Anfield, and this time they slaughtered them 6-0 to win the trophy 7-1 on aggregate.

Birmingham City: Montgomery, Calderwood, Pendrey, Dillon, Howard, Want, Page (Towers), Francis, Bertschin, Hibbitt, Emmanuel.
Nottingham Forest: Shilton, Anderson, Barrett, McGovern, Lloyd, Burns, O'Neill, Gemmill, Withe, Woodcock, Robertson. Sub: Bowyer

Nottingham Forest v. Coventry City

Football League First Division, City Ground
Attendance: 29,823

Date: Saturday 10 December 1977
Referee: Mr J.D. Hough (Macclesfield)

Gordon Milne's free-scoring Coventry had surprised many pundits by reaching fifth place in the table; having said this, the Sky Blues' defence leaked goals like a sieve. The man-to-man marking system that they employed had proved to be quite effective in most of their games, but the opposite in others, particularly in the 6-0 thumping they had received at Everton two weeks earlier. Even so, no one expected them to be a pushover. A young Scot by the name of Ian Wallace, alongside Mick Ferguson, was banging in the goals for the visitors.

Coventry came at Forest right from the off, with Wallace and Ferguson going close with well-struck shots. Woodcock was not about to play second fiddle to the Sky Blues duo, and smacked in a couple of good efforts of his own. Oakey and Coop were doubling up on Robbo, but their close attentions couldn't prevent the Scottish winger from getting over some dangerous crosses, and a stinging shot that Jim Blyth did well to hold on to.

Soon after it was Coventry's turn again. Barrett did well to reach a hospital ball from Burns, and Shilton dived athletically to claw a fierce drive from Nardiello out of the air. Calls for twenty-one-year-old Mick Ferguson to be given a game with the England Under-21 side were understandable, as the big striker gave a marvellous display of how to lead the line, shielding the ball, and playing in his colleagues on numerous occasions, as well as thumping in some dangerous-looking shots. Shilton palmed away a good effort from Tommy Hutchinson, after Ferguson had teed the ball up for the Scottish winger. Then on thirty-nine minutes, Hutchinson fouled Anderson, but chose to mouth-off at the referee, his dispute only earning him a place in the ref's little book. Five minutes before half-time, Martin O'Neill ended Coventry's ascendancy by putting Forest in front with a nicely taken goal. Withe collected the ball and fed Robertson, whose centre eluded Blyth and reached O'Neill at the far post, where the Irishman had the necessary strength to get the ball into the net. This sparked a frenzied five-minute spell.

Back came the Sky Blues for the perfect response. Less than a minute had passed when McDonald sent a free-kick into the box. Up went the heads, but it was Wallace who reached the ball to power a stunning header past Shilton. Withe might not have been scoring, but there is no doubt that his overall contribution was a key factor in Forest's victory. On this occasion, he met a cross from Gemmill, to head on to Woodcock, who beat Blyth, but his swerving shot missed the target. Then Withe teed up Forest's second, feeding the inrushing McGovern, who burst into the box to rifle a left-footed shot beyond Blyth. The ref blew for the break, and the crowd drew a long breath, some needed a Bovril, the rest just needed a rest after a truly breathless finish to the first half!

Understandably, Coventry were a bit miffed to be 2-1 down, and came out for the second period snarling like a pack of wolves. However, despite a few corners and half-chances, they were well contained by a Forest defence with Shilton at his best. The England 'keeper foiled Nardiello and

---

Nottingham Forest 2
O'Neill (40), McGovern (44)

Coventry City 1
Wallace (41)

Martin O'Neill.

Ferguson, before miscuing with a punch that saw the ball drop in front of Wallace. Fortunately Shilts was too quick for the Scottish Under-21 star, diving on the ball to smother the danger.

Blyth wasn't going to be left out, and showed his prowess with a diving catch to keep out Robertson. The Scottish 'keeper then caught a Withe screamer that was heading for the corner of his net. In the closing minutes, with Coventry seriously on the offensive, gaps began to appear at the back, and Blyth had to be extra vigilant to prevent Anderson, Withe and Woodcock from converting good goalscoring opportunities.

The top of the League table after nineteen games:

	PLD	W	D	L	F	A	PTS
Forest	**19**	**13**	**3**	**3**	**34**	**12**	**29**
Everton	19	11	6	2	42	18	28
Liverpool	19	9	5	5	25	15	23
WBA	19	8	7	4	30	22	23
Arsenal	19	9	5	5	23	15	23
Coventry	19	9	5	5	32	29	23

Two clean sheets on the trot; great stuff! Larry Lloyd was struggling with a knock, so Cloughie and Taylor went out and bought unsettled Dave Needham from QPR for £145,000 in time for him to make his debut at Old Trafford. It had been only six months earlier that he had joined Rangers from Notts County. Needham's signing was another masterstroke by the 'Dynamic Duo'.

Oh, I nearly forgot to close the loop on the 'Who would be the new England boss?' saga. Surprise, surprise, the FA appointed caretaker manager Ron Greenwood. His contract would last until July 1980 to correspond with the European Championship finals.

Born in Leicester on 21 May 1949, **Dave Needham** was a highly rated member of Jimmy Sirrell's barnstorming Notts County side of the early 1970s, making 429 League appearances for the Magpies, scoring 32 goals before being transferred to Queens Park Rangers. At QPR Needham made only 18 appearances, scoring 3 goals, when an injury to Larry Lloyd, almost midway through the 1977/78 season, saw Clough dip swiftly into the transfer market to pick up this gem of a footballer. Dave went on to make 81 League appearances for Forest, plus 5 as substitute, weighing in with 9 goals. He missed out on both European Champions Cup finals, and sadly is often remembered for his collision with Peter Shilton during the 1980 League Cup final that allowed Andy Gray to win the trophy for Wolves. In May 1982, Dave was released by Forest, and took up a new challenge in Canada with Toronto Blizzards.

Nottingham Forest: Shilton, Anderson, Barrett, McGovern, Lloyd, Burns, O'Neill, Gemmill, Withe, Woodcock, Robertson. Sub: Bowyer
Coventry City: Blyth, Oakey, Ryan, McDonald, Yorath, Holton, Coop, Nardiello, Wallace, Ferguson, Powell, Hutchison. Sub: Murphy

Manchester United v. Nottingham Forest

Football League First Division, Old Trafford
Attendance: 54,375

Date: Saturday 17 December 1977
Referee: Mr T. Morris (Leeds)

Forest's visit to Old Trafford yielded yet another four-goal victory, to add to the five other games in which Forest had scored four or more goals. Dave Sexton's United started brightly, and had the best of the early exchanges. A great ball from Steve Coppell put Gordon Hill away, the mercurial winger speeding down the left wing to send over a cross that Pearson helped on to Lou Macari, who prodded the ball wide. Then Hill beat Anderson again to whip in another dangerous centre that Dave Needham put behind for a corner. Shilton was happy to fist away Hill's inswinger before Pearson could reach it. However United's centre forward was injured in the collision, and needed copious use of the cold sponge before being able to continue. Forest were certainly under the cosh at this time.

At last they managed to break out, but Withe jumped into Roche, then Woodcock forced a corner, which Robertson swung over. The ball hit a defender then bounced off a Forest player, ricocheting into the air dangerously. Burns soared high to head towards goal, but it was an easy catch for Roche. Needham was booked in the seventeenth minute after he had unceremoniously hauled down Jimmy Greenhoff. Forest went ahead in the twenty-third minute from an own goal by Brian Greenhoff. Withe and Robertson linked up well on the left, before the latter whipped in a cross that eluded Buchan, who maybe should have cleared. The ball found Woodcock on the right of the area and the striker's shot hit the foot of the post, but fortunately bounced into the net off Greenhoff.

Minutes later, Ashley Grimes replaced the limping Stuart Pearson, and the substitute was quickly in the action, getting the ball to Hill, whose first-time effort was well saved by Shilts. All in one movement Shilton punted a long clearance upfield that found Robertson, who sent in a low centre for Woodcock to smash past Roche to put the Reds two up. And with a little more composure, it might well have been three or four-nil within a few minutes. First, Viv Anderson darted in to blast a shot that would surely have broken the net had it been on target. Then, before Anderson repeated his surging run to finish with a left-foot shot, Woodcock swivelled on the spot and hit a near-post shot that was saved by Roche. United should have grabbed a lifeline in injury time, but Jimmy Greenhoff flashed his point-blank header over the bar. Two-nil at half-time was fabulous.

Despite one or two long-range shots from United, Forest were now well on top, McGovern and Gemmill controlling the midfield with comparative ease. On fifty-three minutes, Gemmill set up Forest's third. The Scot's pace took him clear of United's midfielders, and with Buchan coming to meet him, played a near-perfect ball into the path of Robertson. Robbo enticed Roche from his line, before sidestepping the United 'keeper to slide the ball home. A number of chances were created, each looking like producing a fourth goal. A melee in the United goalmouth eventually provided a

---

Manchester United 0

Nottingham Forest 4
Greenhoff (23, own goal),
Woodcock 2 (28, 89), Robertson (53)

MANCHESTER UNITED v. NOTTINGHAM FOREST

Dave Needham.

half-chance for Barrett, but the young full-back could only ponder on the deflection that took the ball wide of the post. With a minute left on the clock, Archie Gemmill's slide-rule pass split the United defence completely, for Woodcock to tap the ball home from close-range. Four-nil to Forest.

If this game had been played today, Forest's travelling band of supporters would have been singing, 'Can we play you every week?' Towards the end of the game the United fans began to chant, 'Sexton out!' A bit mean-spirited I reckon.

Christmas had come early. Forest had another two points. Now for the other Reds – well, after a turkey dinner and a drop of ale.

The top of the League table after twenty games:

	PLD	W	D	L	F	A	PTS
Forest	**20**	**14**	**3**	**3**	**38**	**12**	**31**
Everton	20	11	7	2	42	18	29
Liverpool	20	10	5	5	26	15	25
WBA	20	9	7	4	31	22	25
Arsenal	20	10	5	5	25	16	25
Leeds	20	8	8	4	32	25	24

Manchester Utd: Roche, Nicholl, Houston; McIlroy, Greenhoff B., Buchan, Coppell, Greenhoff J., Pearson Grimes), Macari, Hill.
Nottingham Forest: Shilton, Anderson, Barrett, McGovern, Needham, Burns, O'Neill, Gemmill, Withe, Woodcock, Robertson. Sub: Bowyer

Nottingham Forest v. Liverpool

Football League First Division, City Ground
Date: Boxing Day, Monday 26 December 1977
Attendance: 47,218
Referee: Mr D.W. Civil (Birmingham)

Liverpool were the current League Champions, having won the First Division title in each of the previous two seasons, plus they were current holders of the European Cup, and more recently the 'Super Cup.' So they were going to present a tough test. Even without Kevin Keegan, who had been sold to Bundesliga club Hamburg, they were still formidable contenders for a third successive League title. By the way, Keegan's replacement was a certain Kenny Dalglish; he had cost a staggering £400,000 from Celtic in August 1977. The massive crowd of over 47,000 were treated to an exciting ninety-minute display of committed football, from two of the top teams in England.

Forest applied the pressure from the start, with John Robertson making a series of dangerous runs down the left to cause all manner of problems for England full-back Phil Neal. The Reds' tormentor in chief was aided and abetted by the superb running of Tony Woodcock, and there is no doubt that Liverpool could feel themselves lucky to hold out in the face of Forest's tremendous barrage. In the twenty-first minute, Forest got the breakthrough that their outstanding play deserved. Viv Anderson galloped forward, before slipping the ball to Archie Gemmill, who in turn whipped in a ferocious low drive that flew past the diving Ray Clemence into the far corner of the net. It was a fabulous goal at the end of a move of stunning quality.

Minutes later, a second goal for Forest looked odds-on. John McGovern and Peter Withe passed their way through 'Pool's defence to set up a great chance for Colin Barrett following up their run, but unfortunately, the final ball wasn't good enough and Liverpool breathed a sigh of relief. The pace of play, in particular that of Forest, was simply breathtaking; the skills on show delighting the City Ground crowd. Both defences, determined not to be outdone by the brilliance of the attackers, shone brightly on this cold December day, but none sparkled more than the superb Kenny Burns, who simply oozed class. Alongside Kenny, home-debut boy Dave Needham did more than okay.

Then the worst happened: Liverpool scored. Bob Paisley's side had drawn on their vast experience to mount a spirited comeback, and got their reward when Steve Heighway slotted home the equaliser. It was a goal that would have had Cloughie foaming at the mouth. A harmless-looking right-wing raid was not defended with anywhere near enough determination, and when the ball came across, Heighway darted in to push it home from close range. A bit of a daft goal really, the ball should have been cleared before it reached the Liverpool player. At half-time, the score was 1-1.

The second half was a bit of a let down after the cut and thrust of the first period, and was mostly played in the middle of the park. Neither attack was able to find the kind of devastating form that was seen in abundance in the first period. If Peter Shilton or Ray Clemence had hoped to impress the England manager with their goalkeeping exploits, they would have been tremendously disappointed, for neither one of them had much to do all afternoon. Of course Forest fans needed no convincing as to who was the best 'keeper in England; it was obviously Peter Shilton.

Nottingham Forest 1
Gemmill (21)

Liverpool 1
Heighway (39)

Liverpool's Phil Thompson shields the ball from John McGovern.

Near the end of the game, Forest rediscovered their attacking cohesion and swept downfield to assault the Liverpool goal. Feeding on a defence-splitting through ball, Tony Woodcock raced into the area, where he was clumsily bundled over from behind by Ray Kennedy. Penalty! Got to be! The referee was having none of it, and waved play on. His name might have been Civil, but he certainly didn't live up to it from Forest's point of view. What a swizz! So a draw it finished. Honours were just about even in this top-of-the-table clash, but only in points, because Forest were unlucky not to get both of them.

The news that Everton had been thumped 6-2 at home by Manchester United was music to Forest and their fans, as well as those on the red side of Merseyside. The Toffees followed up this dismal performance with a 3-1 defeat at Leeds the following day. Now there was some daylight showing between Forest and their main challengers.

Nottingham Forest: Shilton, Anderson, Barrett, McGovern, Needham, Burns, O'Neill, Gemmill, Withe, Woodcock, Robertson. Sub: Bowyer
Liverpool: Clemence, Neal, Jones, Thompson P., Kennedy, Hughes, Dalglish, McDermott, Heighway, Fairclough, Case (Callaghan).

Newcastle United v. Nottingham Forest

Football League First Division, St James' Park **Date:** Wednesday 28 December 1977
Attendance: 40,735 **Referee:** Mr D. Richardson (Great Harwood)

New Toon manager Bill McGarry had been installed on 8 November, and was still hoping to work a miracle. They had won their first three games in December, but came into this game on the back of a 4-0 drubbing at Manchester City. The 'other' Magpies had lost thirteen of their first twenty games. Cloughie hoped to make it fourteen with Forest's seventh away win of the campaign.

Forest were pretty much at full strength, and boy did it show, as with this 2-0 win the Reds opened up a five-point lead at the top of the table without having to break sweat. With the game just past the quarter-hour mark, Forest emphasized the huge gulf in class between the two protagonists with a well-rehearsed move. Robbo dropped his accurately placed sixteenth-minute left-wing corner right on the head of Dave Needham, meeting the Forest defender's near-post run perfectly. A smart back-header into the far corner did the rest.

How Forest didn't score a load more goals was a minor miracle in itself. Goalkeeper Kevin Carr dived bravely at Peter Withe's feet to smother the ball, then Tommy Cassidy flung his body in the way of a Tony Woodcock piledriver. Soon after, Martin O'Neill was denied by the woodwork when he went round left-back Allan Barker and angled his run inside the box towards the byline, before whipping in a tremendous drive that spun out off the outside of the post. Just after this near miss, Colin Barrett smashed in a great shot that flew narrowly wide. Newcastle did manage an attempt, but when Tommy Craig sent in a shot that skidded off the surface, there was the commanding Peter Shilton to gather the ball comfortably. When Micky Burns wriggled his way through, England's number one dived at the former Blackpool forward's feet, and the moment of danger passed. Half-time: 1-0 to Forest.

Peter Withe had taken a knock in the first period, Ian Bowyer taking over after the interval, as Forest resumed their quest for more goals. Viv Anderson was left to rue a good chance when his header was scrambled clear by the Newcastle defence. Archie Gemmill looked odds-on to make it two when he surged through to hit a powerful drive, but it unfortunately passed the wrong side of the post. The large partisan Geordie crowd urged their side to even greater efforts, and were almost rewarded when teenager Stuart Robinson crashed in a left-foot shot that flew across the face of Shilton's goal, to miss the far post by a few inches. Then defender John Bird made a foray upfield to try his luck. Thankfully, Dave Needham managed to get in a block on his volley.

That was just about it from Newcastle, and from then on Forest dominated the remainder of the game. Woodcock almost added a second after beating Irving Nattrass, but his fine rising drive crashed against the woodwork; surely Forest must score again soon. And they did. John McGovern waltzed his way into the area to latch onto O'Neill's thoughtful pass. A slight body swerve to the right preceded an explosive shot that deflected past young 'keeper Carr to silence the home crowd. As the game drew to a close, Bowyer took a nasty bang on the head that forced him to leave the

---

Newcastle United 0 **Nottingham Forest 2**
 Needham (16), McGovern (71)

John McGovern.

field for treatment. The other head in the collision belonged to John Bird, who also left the field moments later. Eventually they both returned, but by then the game as a contest was over.

A great result and another competent performance by Forest, without needing to reach the same outstanding level of play that had destroyed Manchester United in their previous away match.

Next day, Bill McGarry splashed out some hefty money on two Scottish strikers, £150,000 on Mark McGhee from First Division Morton, and £100,000 on Mark Larnach from Premier Division Clydebank. McGarry hoped these two would provide the goals to fire Newcastle away from the relegation area. Larnach had only scored 5 goals in league and cup, McGhee had been a little more productive, having scored 17 goals in all competitions. Postscript: Bill's tactical purchases didn't do the trick. McGhee only managed 3 goals in 17 starts, and poor old Larnach didn't even get one in twelve. Morton were promoted to the Scottish Premier Division, but Clydebank lost their premier status, being relegated to the First Division.

The top of the League table after twenty-two games:

	PLD	W	D	L	F	A	PTS
Forest	**22**	**15**	**4**	**3**	**41**	**13**	**34**
Everton	22	11	7	4	45	27	29
Arsenal	22	12	5	5	31	17	29
Liverpool	22	11	6	5	28	16	28
Man City	22	11	4	7	42	24	26
Leeds	22	9	8	5	36	29	26

Five points clear at the top of the table, Forest's next game would be in the West Country. Let's hope the cider would taste sweet.

Forest's captain, **John McGovern** was undoubtedly a favourite of Brian Clough, playing for him at Hartlepool, Derby and Leeds, before arriving at Forest from Leeds United in February 1975, shortly after the great man. A gritty and talented although unspectacular midfielder, he turned out 253 times in League games for Forest, in the process scoring 6 goals. John was born in the Scottish town of Montrose on 28 October 1949, and left Forest for Bolton Wanderers in June 1982. He went on to manage Bolton, Hull City and Ilkeston Town, before working as a summariser for BBC Radio Nottingham.

Newcastle United: Carr, Nattrass, Barker, Cassidy, Bird, Blackhall, Martin, Burns M., Cannell (Barrowclough), Craig T., Robinson.

Nottingham Forest: Shilton, Anderson, Barrett, McGovern, Needham, Burns, O'Neill, Gemmill, Withe (Bowyer), Woodcock, Robertson.

BRISTOL CITY v. NOTTINGHAM FOREST

Football League First Division, Ashton Gate
Attendance: 31,990

Date: New Year's Eve, Saturday 31 December 1977
Referee: Mr L. Shapter (Newton Abbott)

In front of a capacity crowd at Ashton Gate, Forest saw out the old year in style. The gates were closed twenty minutes before kick-off, with hordes of West Country folk wanting to see how their team might fair against the League leaders now that they had signed Joe Royle from Manchester City for £90,000.

Forest almost went one down in the first minute when Dave Needham launched himself at a Tainton free-kick, to power the ball past the angle of his own goal for a corner. The danger was still in evidence as the ball came over. Collier leapt highest to head back into the middle, where the Forest defenders were pleased to see Gillies's first-time effort pass wide of the upright. A time to draw breath? For a time, Forest played keep-ball as they calmed down the proceedings, before moving slickly up a few gears to put the pressure on the home side. In their first attack, Gemmill found Woodcock in a menacing position, and it was the Robins' turn to be happy to concede a corner.

Robbo played the ball to the head of the inrushing Anderson, which had Shaw stretching to make a fine catch. Then Forest got the all-important first goal through Dave Needham, his second in successive games. The referee penalised Collier for a foul, and Needham darted in to meet Withe's chip, to place a brilliant header wide of the diving Shaw. Needham was beginning to look a fabulous buy, and again caused a panic in the City box. This time he was only inches away from converting Gemmill's free-kick, Joe Royle fractionally beating him to the ball. City were having trouble getting past Forest's midfield, and goalkeeper Shaw again had to be alert, diving at full stretch to his right to keep out a fierce Barrett shot. Then Forest went two up.

Martin O'Neill drifted into space on the right, and dinked the ball to Gemmill, who ran on a few yards, before cracking in a fabulous rising shot that cannoned off the bar into the path of Tony Woodcock, who had the simplest of tasks to put the ball over the line. Before half-time, Needham repeated his earlier mistake as again his defensive header brushed the angle of bar and post. At the other end Shaw denied Woodcock when the Forest striker looked certain to make it 3-0 and Forest had to make do with a 2-0 lead at the break.

In the second half, Forest had chances in abundance and should have stitched up the Robins like a kipper. Anderson was set up by the combination of Withe and Woodcock, but narrowly missed the target. Suddenly City came alive. Finding the will to abandon their defensive strategy, which was obviously not working, they now attacked in force. Merrick got in a fine cross, which Joe Royle headed down to Ritchie, who smacked the ball into the net. However, City's celebrations were immediately halted by the referee, who explained that the striker had been miles offside. Withe missed another gilt-edged chance to put his goalscoring problems behind him. One goal in his last thirteen League games was not a good return for a top striker. Then O'Neill rifled in a shot that was smothered by Shaw, before grabbing a third for the Reds in the fifty-eighth minute.

Bristol City 1
    Mabbutt (82)

Nottingham Forest 3
    Needham (11), Woodcock (21),
    O'Neill (58)

Bristol City v. Nottingham Forest

I suppose when you are 3-0 up away from home, a natural tendency to lift the foot slightly off the pedal is understandable, and that is exactly what Forest did now. Regrettably they got punished for it. In the final ten minutes of the game, Kevin Mabbutt came on for Donnie Gillies as City threw all they had at their visitors. Two minutes later, Joe Royle headed the ball on to Mabbutt, who had stolen in behind the Forest defence. The Red's defenders all stopped, expecting the ref to blow for offside, allowing the young striker to pick his spot with a fierce rising drive past Shilton into the top corner, a fine consolation goal.

They nearly got a second, again through the lively Mabbutt, who sent in a ferocious shot that swerved viciously towards Shilton's top corner. Fortunately, Shilts was wide awake and sprang across to make the save. Then he had to be on his toes to push behind a left-foot screamer from the same player. It was a strong finish by the Robins, but in reality too late.

Peter Withe had now gone six games without scoring; thank goodness goals were coming from midfield and defence.

Three games in a week had resulted in 5 points out of 6. The Championship was now looking very much like a two-horse race between Forest and Everton, who strangely enough were Forest's next opponents in what was the Reds' fourth game in eight days. The Reds had already been installed as the bookies' favourite. The odds were now even-money on Forest winning the League title.

Brian Clough gave **Kenny Burns** the night off from the final League game of the 1977/78 season to allow him to pick up his Footballer of the Year award at the soccer writers' dinner in London. The one-time bad-boy striker-cum-defender of Birmingham City, now reformed at Nottingham Forest, thoroughly deserved his accolade. Clough had seen the talent and the temperament of Kenny Burns, already capped by Scotland at centre forward, and had decided he was the man for him. He got his man for a measly £150,000. Most football pundits thought him mad, even at that price, but as usual, Clough ignored them, confident he could turn this Scot into a world-class defender. And he was right. Burns was selected for Scotland's World Cup squad as a central defender at the end of his first full season playing in defence. Born in Glasgow on 23 September 1953, Scottish international Kenny Burns was a solid defender, hard, but skilful. His reputation of being short on discipline was reversed at Forest. He was only booked once in Forest's League Championship season, and that was for time-wasting. He went on to win 20 caps for his country, scoring 1 goal, to go with all his other achievements. In a fairly short career with Forest, Kenny Burns made 137 League appearances for the Reds, scoring 13 goals, and was transferred to Leeds United in October 1981, and subsequently to Derby County.

Bristol City: Shaw, Sweeney, Merrick, Gow, Collier, Hunter, Tainton, Ritchie, Royle, Gillies (Mabbutt), Mann.
Nottingham Forest: Shilton, Anderson, Barrett, McGovern, Needham, Burns, O'Neill, Gemmill, Withe, Woodcock, Robertson. Sub: O'Hare

NOTTINGHAM FOREST v. EVERTON

Football League First Division, City Ground
Attendance: 44,030

Date: Monday 2 January 1978
Referee: Mr R.W. Toseland (Kettering)

Forest started the New Year with this hard-fought draw against one of their closest rivals for the Championship, courtesy of a John Robertson penalty. However, the game was full of controversy, mostly created by referee Ray Toseland, who, let's say, made one or two odd decisions.

In the first quarter of an hour of this absorbing contest Everton's defenders had kept Forest's attack under control, and although at the other end it was a similar story with Needham and Burns well on top of Latchford and McKenzie, the best chances of the early exchanges fell to Everton. Trevor Ross brought a fabulous diving save from Shilton, before Martin Dobson watched his rising drive clear the crossbar. Then disaster struck for the Toffees in the twenty-fifth minute when the referee gave Forest a penalty after what appeared to be a coming together of a number of players. It's probably fair to say that his decision looked a trifle harsh even to the most partisan Reds' fan. However, it's daft to look a gift horse in the mouth, and Robbo stepped up to hammer the ball past George Wood. That the decision stunned the Toffees is an understatement, and that in itself enabled Forest to pile on a bit of pressure, without too much to show for their efforts.

After the break, Forest renewed their efforts to double their goal tally, and now Everton had cause to say a big thank you to Lady Luck. Much to the chagrin of the huge holiday crowd, referee Toseland chalked off goals from Dave Needham and Martin O'Neill. Some even questioned Toseland's myopic condition as well as his parentage, especially when Terry Darracott tripped Robbo in the box. It certainly looked suspiciously like a penalty. The Everton full-back had already been booked in the first half for bringing down Robbo. 'Play on' was the decision.

Next it was Peter Withe's turn to test the Everton goalkeeper. Forest's number nine fired in a tremendous left-foot scorcher that Wood reached at full stretch to fist clear. In the seventy-fifth minute, John McGovern swept through Everton's defence, looking odds-on to score before Wood, at full stretch clawed away the skipper's goal-bound shot, and Pejic completed the clearance. Forest were unlucky not to find themselves two or three up, when Mr Toseland took a hand in the proceedings once again. With only five minutes left on the clock Duncan McKenzie managed to get on the end of an innocuous-looking corner, to head towards goal. According to the ref, the ball was handled by Kenny Burns, and the man in black pointed to the spot. It was a tenuous allegation to say the least, but despite the protests of the Forest players, the official stood his ground, and Trevor Ross slotted the ball past Shilton. Everton's players were jubilant; they knew that the referee had got them out of jail.

This was undoubtedly a game that Forest should have won, despite the visitors' skilful midfield play, but at least they didn't lose. Forest old boy Duncan McKenzie showed a couple of flashes of the skill that used to have the City Ground crowd purring. The League's top scorer Bob Latchford was well shackled by Kenny Burns and Needham.

Nottingham Forest 1
Robertson (penalty 25)

Everton 1
Ross (penalty 85)

Nottingham Forest v. Everton

John Robertson.

Referee Toseland went back to Kettering unrepentant, saying that he was satisfied that he had made the correct decisions, and that he had no hesitation in giving the penalties, 'There was clearly pushing for the first one, and I was convinced Burns handled for the second.' Was he convinced, or merely attempting to convince himself? Whatever he thought, nothing would change the result now.

On 2 January we learned that the FA had appointed Clough and Taylor, along with Ken Burton, to look after the England youth team.

Some big transfers dominated the football news, the most notable being Joe Jordan moving to Manchester United from Leeds for a fee reported to be £350,000, and Liverpool's signing of midfielder Graeme Souness from Middlesbrough for £352,000.

Nottingham Forest: Shilton, Anderson, Barrett, McGovern, Needham, Burns, O'Neill, Gemmill, Withe, Woodcock, Robertson. Sub: O'Hare
Everton: Wood, Darracott, Pejic, Lyons, Kenyon (Jones), Ross, King, Dobson, Latchford, McKenzie, Thomas.

Nottingham Forest v. Swindon Town

FA Cup third round, City Ground
Attendance: 28,953

Date: Saturday 7 January 1978
Referee: Mr K.W. Baker (Rugby)

Forest cruised into the fourth round of the FA Cup with this easy win. Tony Woodcock notched his twelfth and thirteenth goals in all competitions, and Peter Withe scored again at last; also his thirteenth of the season.

Third Division Swindon gave Forest few difficulties in a game that emphasised the huge gulf in class between the two sides. That said, the Robins fought hard and valiantly, and even scored a consolation goal in a dogged performance. However, they were rolled over by four outstanding strikes on goal, from which there really was no coming back. Swindon's usual left-back Trollope played on the right-hand side after being detailed to curb the threat of Robertson. That he failed to do this, as indeed so many already had, was no shame on this long-serving player. With only a minute gone, Robbo eased his way along the left wing, before finding Peter Withe with a neat pass, who in turn, reversed the ball to Colin Barrett. The young full-back thumped in a shot that came back to him off a defender, and Swindon somehow scrambled the ball to safety.

Forest had given notice of how they would approach this game, emphasised again a minute later, when Robertson spanked in a great effort that whizzed past the angle of post and bar. The Robins' only response was a speculative long-range shot from Ray McHale that was miles off target, then goalkeeper Jimmy Allan was injured when he had to sprint from his line to smother O'Neill's through ball as it reached Woodcock. After this, the Reds were a bit rushed in their early play, no doubt wanting to get the job done as quickly as possible, but it wasn't until the thirty-seventh minute that their possession and power play penetrated a resolute Swindon defence. Anderson carved his way into the heart of the Swindon defence to slip the ball to Withe. The big number nine pushed a neat pass to Woodcock, who placed the ball well wide of Allan to put Forest ahead. In the intervening period until half-time, Allan pulled off a number of fine saves to deny the Reds a second goal. Shilton too, had a couple of efforts to deal with. Then the referee refused to accept Robertson's penalty appeal. As he saw it, the ball had struck Ken Stroud's body, not his arm.

After the break, Kenny Burns tried a long-range effort. Then found himself back-pedalling as Swindon broke down the right, the move bringing a free-kick. Dave Moss, hoping to catch Shilton off guard, clipped the ball to the near post, where Shilts dived to turn it round the post. From the resultant corner, a mass of players jumped to meet John McLaughlin's centre, but Peter Withe was first to the ball to head clear. Back came the Robins, attackers outnumbering defenders. Unfortunately, for the visitors, Chris Kamara found himself with too much time and in too much space, and finally blazed harmlessly over. Seconds later, McGovern was flattened by Kamara, who was rightly booked for the offence; maybe there was a hint of frustration involved. Swindon then made a change, Lewis replacing Guthrie.

Nottingham Forest 4
   Woodcock 2 (37, 77),
   Withe (55), Robertson (67)

Swindon Town 1
   Moss (84)

Forest weren't yet in a position to relax at all, but ten minutes of play in the second period changed all that. In the fifty-fifth minute, the ball was fed to O'Neill, whose swinging cross was headed down by Woodcock, for Withe to finally get his name on the scoresheet again. The striker put all his pent-up frustration into his shot as he quite literally smashed the ball into the net. The relief on his face was there for all to see. Swindon knew that they had to throw caution to the wind, and renewed their assault on the Forest goal. A quick free-kick forced Shilton to dive full length to paw the ball away after Burns' attempted clearance had found Ford. Just after Barrett's header had skimmed a post, Robertson scored a great solo goal. Collecting the ball on the left, the Scot turned Trollope inside out, before whipping in a stinging shot from an acute angle to make it 3-0.

John O'Hare was called into the action to replace Peter Withe, and in the seventy-seventh minute, a piece of excellent play from the powerful Scot set up a fourth for Forest. The barrel-chested substitute controlled the ball magnificently before playing in Woodcock, whose first-time thunderbolt flew past the helpless Allan. Still Swindon wouldn't lie down. McHale forced Shilton to tip his rising drive over the bar, then Kamara put a header straight into Shilton's arms; it just wasn't their day. At least their fans had something to cheer them up on the way back to Wiltshire when Dave Moss made it 4-1 with a goal six minutes from time.

Time for another Ram-raid?

Tony Woodcock was born in Nottingham on 6 December 1955, and signed apprentice forms for Forest in January 1974, making his first-team debut on 24 April 1974 in the 3-1 defeat by Aston Villa at Villa Park in the penultimate game of the season. He also played in the final game, a 2-0 win away at Portsmouth. In the following season, 1974/75, he made 5 appearances, plus 4 as substitute, but didn't score in any of these games. He was then loaned out to Doncaster and Lincoln City to hone his goalscoring technique and his confidence. He returned to the Forest side on 6 November 1976, getting his first senior goal one week later in the 1-0 win at Orient, going on to score 11 League goals in 30 appearances in that promotion-winning season. In all he made 125 League appearances for Forest, plus 4 as substitute, scoring 36 League goals.

The PFA's Young Player of the Year in 1978, Woodcock won 42 caps for England, scoring 16 goals. A bit surprisingly, Clough sold him to German Bundesliga side Cologne in November 1979, the club that Forest beat 4-3 on aggregate in the semi-finals of the European Cup in April 1979; they must have liked what they saw. He subsequently transferred to Arsenal in July 1982.

Opposite: Tony Woodcock.

Nottingham Forest: Shilton, Anderson, Barrett, McGovern, Needham, Burns, O'Neill, Gemmill, Withe (O'Hare), Woodcock, Robertson.
Swindon Town: Allan, McLaughlin, Trollope, Ford, Kamara, Prophett, Moss, Stroud, Guthrie (Lewis), McHale, Cunningham.

DERBY COUNTY V. NOTTINGHAM FOREST

Football League First Division, Baseball Ground   **Date:** Saturday 14 January 1978
Attendance: 36,500   **Referee:** Mr D. Turner (Cannock)

This was a game for 'old boys.' Forest had Archie Gemmill (ex-Derby), and the Rams had ex-Reds John Middleton and Terry Curran, the latter having been sold to Derby in the previous November after being loaned out to Bury. Unfortunately, the goal spark that the massive crowd might have expected this fixture to generate was sadly never more than a dull glow. Having said that, the action at times was frenetic, with a plethora of dangerous shots raining in at both ends. The two goalkeepers on show both gave faultless displays of their art.

Derby had Bruce Rioch, a £150,000 October signing from Everton, in midfield, but it was Forest that showed first, with Woodcock latching onto a pass after Buckley had given away a free-kick for pulling down Anderson. The youngster received the ball and sent in a low shot that beat Middleton, but was scrambled away by a Derby defender. Scottish midfielder Rioch showed his power with three good strikes on goal in a five-minute spell of Derby pressure. The first came after Charlie George had reversed a pass to him, which he dispatched just outside the top of the upright with his left foot. Former Forest winger Curran tricked his way around Barrett before hitting a shot that forced Shilton to get down smartly to keep the ball out. Then Rioch smashed in a ferocious volley that Shilton turned around the post in classic style. Rioch seemed determined to score, and a minute later whipped in a stinging right-footer that skimmed the far post.

Forest came back at Derby with a vengeance, besieging the Rams' goal that somehow survived intact. Robertson forced a corner, which Woodcock took, swinging in a great ball that Barrett met perfectly, or so it seemed until it smacked against the post. The rebound carried it as far as Robertson, whose first-time shot was blocked on the line before being scrambled away.

Now the Rams hit back. Rioch's searching pass found Curran on the other flank, and the winger made ground before crossing the ball to Charlie George. However, the ex-Arsenal star could only watch in horror as Shilton pulled off a magnificent save. Terry Curran looked like he had something to prove to the Forest management team, and again looked dangerous as he delivered a cross from the byline that was put out for a corner, which was eventually cleared. Then minutes later Shilton raced off his line to block a shot from Daly, after he had been put through by George. In the Derby goal, Middleton emulated Shilton's skill to block a stinging effort by Martin O'Neill.

At the referee's whistle signalling half-time, both sides were enthusiastically applauded from the pitch. A reoccurrence of Gerry Ryan's hamstring injury caused him to be substituted by Steve Powell at the interval. The second period was a repeat of the first, lightning attacks meeting dogged defending. The first strike of the half went to the Rams, Charlie George firing just over, before an injury to Kenny Burns' knee caused a lengthy delay while he received attention. Then a snap shot from Tony Woodcock flew way over, and Daniel was booked for bringing down Gemmill. However, Robbo's low free-kick was scrambled away, although not without difficulty. From

Derby County 0   Nottingham Forest 0

another Robertson free-kick, Dave Needham shook the bar with a powerful header with Middleton beaten all ends up.

There were a number of scares at Shilton's end of the ground. Rioch fired wide left, and then, wide right, Powell volleyed past, and Curran whipped in a right-foot effort that was booted away. Not to be outdone, Barrett and Woodcock combined down the left. The ball was played to Withe whose wickedly deflected shot looked to be heading for the top corner until Middleton, at full stretch, clawed the ball away. It was breathtaking stuff, of that there can be no doubt, and I suppose that in the end, 0-0 was an equitable result.

The top four in the table after twenty-five League games:

	PLD	W	D	L	F	A	PTS
Forest	**25**	**16**	**6**	**3**	**45**	**15**	**38**
Everton	25	13	8	4	49	28	34
Liverpool	25	14	6	5	33	16	34
Arsenal	25	14	5	6	35	20	33

Bob Latchford of Everton led the scoring charts with 20 goals to his name from 25 starts; Ian Wallace of Coventry, with 15 goals, was his nearest rival for the £10,000 prize offered by the *Daily Express* for the first striker to reach 30 League goals in the season.

Four days after not quite disposing of the Rams, it was back to League Cup action, to meet Third Division Bury, who had surprisingly beaten West Brom 1-0 to reach the quarter-finals.

Garry Birtles was transferred to Manchester United for a reputed £1.25 million in October 1980, scoring 11 goals in 57 appearances, plus one as substitute for the Red Devils, helping them to a third-place finish in 1980/81. He returned to the City Ground in September 1982 when Brian Clough bought him back for around £275,000. In 1985/86 Birtles was successfully converted to a central defender for a time, but subsequently resumed his striking role to forge a strong partnership with the young Nigel Clough in 1986/87. In June 1987 Garry was given a free-transfer and made the short journey across the Trent to join the Magpies, where the majority of his appearances were at centre-half. He moved from Meadow Lane to Grimsby Town on a free in July 1989 and stayed until May 1992, joining Ilkeston Town on a free in August 1992. Garry was assistant-manager to Paul Futcher at Gresley Rovers in season 1993/94 before taking over as manager for the following season. Now pursuing a career in the media with Century 106 fm and Sky Television, also writing for the Nottingham Evening Post. For Nottingham Forest Garry made a total of 278 appearances, 5 as substitute, scoring a total of 96 goals in all competitions. Also winning 3 full England caps, to add to his two at Under-21 and one for England 'B.' In 1978/79 season he was voted 'Young Player of the Year' by the Midland Sports Writers and was also 'Young European Footballer of the Year' in 1978.

Derby County: Middleton, Langan, Buckley, Rioch, Daniel, Todd, Curran, Daly G., Masson, George, Ryan (Powell S,).

Nottingham Forest: Shilton, Anderson, Barrett, McGovern, Needham, Burns, O'Neill, Gemmill, Withe, Woodcock, Robertson. Sub: Bowyer

BURY v. NOTTINGHAM FOREST

Football League Cup quarter-final, Gigg Lane
Attendance: 21,500

Date: Tuesday 17 January 1978
Referee: Mr K. Styles (Barnsley)

Forest's first away tie in this competition went the way of the first two rounds, only this time against lowly opposition in the form of Third Division Bury they only managed to score three. John Robertson got his ninth of the season, Ian Bowyer his eighth, five of those coming in this competition. Chris Woods was again selected in goal, with Colin Barrett alongside Kenny Burns at the heart of the defence, and Frank Clark returning for his first start since the previous September. All slotted in superbly.

There was no way that Forest were going to let Bob Stokoe's boys repeat their victory over the Baggies, and they attacked from the first whistle. In the eighth minute came the first goal. Peter Withe outjumped the Bury defence to head Robertson's corner for goal. The ball bounced kindly off a Bury defender and Ian Bowyer rammed it home. Only some dogged defending by the Lancashire side kept the score at one. Tony Woodcock was unlucky to have a fine volleyed goal disallowed by the referee, who ruled that Frank Clark had been guilty of pushing as he headed the ball down to the young striker. Then Viv Anderson beat the Bury offside trap to race onto a great ball from Burns. Spotting Colin Barrett racing in at the near post, Forest's number two slid the ball into his path, only to hold his head as Barrett spooned his shot over the bar.

Shortly after, John Forrest dived at full stretch to pull down a fierce low shot from Ian Bowyer, and then after O'Neill had set up a chance, the Bury 'keeper prevented McGovern putting his name on the scoresheet with an instinctive save. Bury did manage a couple of efforts on goal, but each time Chris Woods was equal to the task. The best effort was a snap shot from Ian Robins that Woods made look easy as he fielded the ball. Half-time: 1-0 to Forest.

Ten minutes after the restart Bowyer started the move that led to Forest's second with a long raking pass across the field to Martin O'Neill that Bury defender John Kennedy missed completely. O'Neill powered his way into the box before unleashing an unstoppable shot wide of John Forrest's dive. It took Forest a long time to fashion a third goal, but in the intervening minutes worked a number of good situations that unfortunately came to nothing.

With twelve minutes of the game remaining, and with Bury on the attack, there seemed little danger when Bowyer played a long ball out of defence to Robbo. However, the Shakers' defenders hadn't done their homework as the Scottish winger started a run from just inside his own half. Some of the defenders in front of him backed away leaving space for Robbo to run into. By the time they realised the danger, he was near the area and as they moved to force him wide he easily sidestepped and veered towards goal before unleashing a rising thunderbolt that cannoned into the net off the underside of the bar. It was a goal of sheer quality to cap a fantastic virtuoso performance by Forest's left-winger. Near the end, Bury's best chance came when Jimmy McIlwraith put his header over the bar when it seemed easier to score. This was Forest's night by a street. Now for the semi-finals.

Bury 0

Nottingham Forest 3
Bowyer (8), O'Neill (55),
Robertson (78)

Martin O'Neill.

Next up was a chance to gain a little revenge for that defeat at Highbury earlier in the season.

Born in Kilrea, Northern Ireland on 1 March 1952, **Martin O'Neill** was signed by Forest in October 1971, and had 10 seasons at the City Ground. He was without doubt, in his heyday, one of the finest right-sided midfield players around, and he made 264 League appearances for Forest, plus 21 as substitute, scoring 48 goals. Martin won 39 caps for Northern Ireland.

Transferred to Norwich for a fee of £250,000 in February 1981, he made only 11 League appearances before moving to Manchester City, and twelve League games later back to Norwich, and then to Notts County. He went on to manage Wycombe Wanderers and Leicester City prior to landing the plum job of manager of Scottish giants Celtic.

Bury: Forrest, Keenan, Kennedy, Hatton, Tucker, Whitehead, Stanton, Thomson, Rowland, Robins, McIlwraith. Sub: Hamstead

Nottingham Forest: Woods, Anderson, Clark, McGovern, Barrett, Burns, O'Neill, Bowyer, Withe, Woodcock, Robertson. Sub: O'Hare

Nottingham Forest v. Arsenal

Football League First Division, City Ground
Attendance: 35,743

Date: Saturday 21 January 1978
Referee: Mr D. Shaw (Sandbach)

This result was sweet revenge for Forest following the 3-0 defeat at Highbury in the fourth game of the campaign. Although the fire had been sparked, it took a while before the game came to life, after the tactics of both teams appeared to be cancelling each other out.

It took the Gunners nearly half an hour to put together a serious attack, but when they did it was stunning to watch. Liam Brady slalomed round a couple of Forest players and caressed an inch-perfect pass to Alan Sunderland. The former Wolves starlet took aim with a low drive that had goal written all over it, until Shilton, diving to his right, stretched the length of his considerable frame to push the ball away. A truly world-class save. Maybe the Gunners should not have tweaked the Forest beard, because Sunderland's effort spurred them into life, and two minutes later they were in front. With O'Neill pressing, Sammy Nelson headed behind for a corner, which Woodcock swerved into the six-yard box for Dave Needham, running in at the near post, to nod the ball past Jennings.

Back came Arsenal, and again Brady found Sunderland unmarked on the right. But from his cross, MacDonald's header skimmed the bar. Then it was big Pat Jennings' turn to keep the score to 1-0. First, he came out bravely to fist away from O'Neill as the Forest midfielder stretched to meet Robbo's cross. Minutes later, Barrett's low shot took a nasty bounce in front of the Irish 'keeper as he was about to gather. The ball flew off his body, but with Woodcock challenging, Jennings managed to grab the ball.

Forest were playing some neat football, with McGovern and Gemmill linking up well with Robertson, resulting in a number of dangerous centres that the Arsenal defenders were pleased to be able to clear. Late in the half, Arsenal forced a couple of corners on the right that might have produced a goal. Graham Rix swung in the first, after Barrett had put the ball behind, and Shilton had to be quick to take the ball from Malcolm MacDonald's head. The second came shortly after. Willie Young was presented with a great chance to bring the scores level, when, after Shilton had uncharacteristically missed the ball, the big Scot's shot hit Withe on the line. Then 'Supermac' cut in from the left to crash a ferocious shot just wide of Shilton's near post. Half-time: Forest one, Arsenal nil.

Arsenal began the second half hell-bent on getting an equaliser. They bombarded Forest's goal with a series of crosses and corners that brought the very best out of Peter Shilton. The towering 'keeper proving equal to all that was thrown at him, although, on a couple of occasions, he did need a little help from his fellow defenders. Again, this seemed to sting Forest into action. The ball was worked out on the left by Robertson, who whipped over a well-aimed centre that Withe nodded down to Woodcock, but his half-hit shot was cleared. Then Forest's number nine played a neat one-two with Robbo that ended in O'Neill heading over Withe's swerving centre. Peter Withe was really getting through a lot of work, and now found O'Neill with a shrewd pass, but

---

Nottingham Forest 2
Needham (32), Gemmill (64)

Arsenal 0

Archie Gemmill.

unfortunately, the Irishman's shot was well wide of the target. Seconds later, Jennings grabbed a stubbed shot from Barrett, and then sailed through the air to push over Barrett's header. Four minutes after the hour mark, Forest created a breathtaking move that brought them a second goal; just reward for all their pressure.

Archie Gemmill fed Withe on the left, who whipped the ball into the Arsenal penalty area, where Gemmill raced in unchallenged to slide the ball past Jennings. After Barrett had produced a great saving tackle, Forest poured onto the attack, and came close to extending their lead. From a long clearance, the ball bounced into the Gunners' box, where Jennings prevented Withe from scoring. Then Jennings bravely dived to push Woodcock's effort for a corner, after Gemmill had cleverly flicked the ball to his young teammate. Jennings' next save was a flying one-hander to keep out a Robertson thunderbolt. Then just before the final whistle, the big Irishman showed why many considered him to be the finest goalkeeper around, by denying Woodcock on two more occasions.

Nottingham Forest v. Arsenal

The top of the League table after twenty-six games:

	PLD	W	D	L	F	A	PTS
Forest	**26**	**17**	**6**	**3**	**47**	**15**	**40**
Man City	26	15	4	7	51	27	34
Everton	26	13	8	5	50	31	34
Liverpool	26	14	6	6	35	19	34
Arsenal	26	14	5	7	35	22	33
Leeds	26	11	8	7	41	34	30

Forest's FA Cup fourth-round tie with Manchester City, scheduled for Saturday 28 January, was a victim of the weather, and had to be rescheduled for the following Tuesday, because of a waterlogged pitch. In a midday inspection of the rain-soaked City Ground pitch, Stourbridge referee Ken Burns took less than a minute to call off the game. He explained, 'The water was over the tops of my ankles, so there is no point in playing a game that would be a lottery.'

The pools panel sat for the first time since 15 January 1977. The panel was called in when twenty-five or more matches on the pools coupon were postponed. The panel consisted of Lord Bath as chairman, former referee Arthur Ellis, plus ex-players Tony Green, Ronnie Simpson, Roger Hunt and Stan Mortensen. Other games that fell victim to the weather: Chelsea v. Burnley, Derby v. Birmingham, Bolton v. Mansfield, Brighton v. Notts County, Millwall v. Luton, and Stoke v. Blyth Spartans. The panel predicted a score draw for Forest. Just shows you what they know, eh?

Elsewhere in the country, large drifts of snow curtailed many a journey. In Scotland, seventy passengers were stranded in a snowbound train for more than four hours, eventually being winched to safety in what was Scotland's biggest combined helicopter rescue operation.

Nottingham Forest: Shilton, Anderson, Barrett, McGovern, Needham, Burns, O'Neill, Gemmill, Withe, Woodcock, Robertson. Sub: Bowyer

Arsenal: Jennings, Rice, Nelson, Price, O'Leary, Young, Brady, Sunderland, MacDonald, Stapleton, Rix. Sub: Matthews

Nottingham Forest v. Manchester City

FA Cup fourth round, City Ground
Attendance: 38,509

Date: Tuesday 31 January 1978
Referee: Mr K. Burns (Stourbridge)

This match, rearranged from the previous Saturday, was a real top-of-the-table clash. First-placed Forest continued their winning ways against second-placed Manchester City, beating them by the same score as their League encounter in October.

The Reds were quite literally magnificent, going ahead in the third minute, after a four-man move set up the chance. Viv Anderson and Kenny Burns played the ball out of defence before finding Tony Woodcock, who brought Peter Withe into the play. Withe hit a defence-splitting pass across the field to John Robertson, who gave the large crowd a repeat of the goal he scored at Bury. Controlling the ball beautifully, Robbo wrong-footed the two defenders that attempted to block his path and then fired in a low right-foot shot that passed between them and into the net just inside the far post, beyond the despairing dive of Joe Corrigan. Another one for the photograph album.

Another great piece of play saw the ball passed to Viv Anderson, who set off on one of his galloping forays up the field to end his brilliant solo run with a stunning left-footer that whistled inches the wrong side of Corrigan's post. Soon after, he did it again, but this time, before he could pull the trigger, Tommy Booth brought him crashing to the ground, a crime for which the City stopper rightly earned a booking. Unfortunately, the free-kick yielded nothing.

Against a team of City's quality there was no way that Forest could continue their dominance without having to defend a few times, and in a quarter of an hour spell before the break, City came back into the game. First, when Forest failed to clear Asa Hartford's free-kick, Dennis Tueart was given far too much time and space to crash in a shot that Peter Shilton dived at full stretch to keep out. Then the Forest 'keeper had to go one better to prevent Brian Kidd from bringing City back into the game. City's midfielders were suddenly running the show, and Forest were glad to hear the referee's whistle signalling half-time.

City played their joker at the start of the second half, bringing on Mike Channon, their £300,000 signing, for Gary Owen. But it was the Reds who produced the first chance of the half through the back-to-form Peter Withe in the forty-sixth minute. It looked odds-on a second goal for Forest when Tony Woodcock ran on to Martin O'Neill's slide-rule pass and left Booth trailing in his wake. Corrigan charged off his line, diving bravely at the striker's feet to block the ball away as Woodcock tried to take it round him. The ball ran loose to Withe, but with the goal gaping somehow the Forest number nine contrived to scoop his effort over the bar: unbelievable!

In Forest's next attack, Woodcock combined well with O'Neill, running intelligently to create an inviting gap that the Irishman ran into before unleashing a tremendous shot that flashed past the post. Then it was Shilton's turn to be a hero, diving at the near post onto Kidd's excellent low shot. Seconds later, a lovely piece of play by Gemmill and O'Neill ended with Peter Withe's thunderbolt

---

Nottingham Forest 2
Robertson (3), Withe (59)

Manchester City 1
Kidd (61)

Nottingham Forest v. Manchester City

John Robertson.

knocking the stuffing out of Dave Watson, who luckily for Corrigan, simply couldn't get out of the way. One minute before the hour mark Forest's domination bore fruit.

Robbo took a short corner on the left, with the ball eventually rebounding back to him off Kenny Clements, City thought he had controlled the ball with his hand or arm, but either way the referee didn't see it, and Forest's winger whipped the ball to the near post where Withe headed it powerfully into the net. It was looking mighty good for the Reds, but then two minutes after Withe's goal, City got one back. Kenny Clements went on a great overlapping run and was found by Tueart with a neat pass. The raiding full-back squared a low cross to Brian Kidd who turned it sweetly past Shilton from ten yards. Oh 'eck! Could the Reds hold out for the final half-hour? Actually they didn't bother to try; instead they went straight for City's jugular.

Joe Corrigan was now in for bit of a hectic time. First he had to dive smartly to push away a shot from Martin O'Neill, and then could only watch helplessly as Peter Withe smacked a low drive against the base of the post. A few minutes later, Woodcock's snap shot beat the 'keeper's despairing dive, but only shaved a bit of paint off the outside of a post. Suddenly, it was all over, and Forest were through to the fifth round. That seemingly impossible dream of 'the treble' was still very much alive and kicking. Although not attracting a capacity crowd, this game did produce a record receipt of £50,000.

This was heady stuff!

On 4 February, the pools panel had to be called in again after the inclement weather played havoc with the League programme. Fortunately, Forest managed to get their game on. It was certainly a little damp, but at least no one had to be sent out for shark repellent!

Nottingham Forest: Shilton, Anderson, Barrett, McGovern, Needham, Burns, O'Neill, Gemmill, Withe, Woodcock, Robertson. Sub: Bowyer

Manchester City: Corrigan, Clements, Donachie, Booth, Watson, Owen (Channon), Barnes, Bell, Kidd, Hartford, Tueart.

Nottingham Forest v. Wolverhampton Wanderers

Football League First Division, City Ground
Attendance: 28,803

Date: Saturday 4 February 1978
Referee: Mr D.T. Richardson (Lincoln)

The City Ground surface was still covered with water when referee Derrick Richardson, who had arrived well before noon, inspected the pitch several times before eventually declaring the pitch playable.

Forest comfortably did the double over Wolves, their colleagues in promotion from the previous season, with Tony Woodcock grabbing his fourteenth goal of the season in all competitions; nine in the League, two in the FA Cup, and three in the League Cup. As in the Arsenal game, this one took some time to get going, and of course, the slippery surface didn't help. Playing the ball along the ground was not a practical option. Five minutes before the interval, Colin Barrett outpaced Geoff Palmer, making a great run, before crossing from the byline. Martin O'Neill, racing in, headed powerfully towards goal. The ball hit a defender and dropped into a crowd of players all swinging at it desperately to hack the ball clear as it stuck in the mud, but it was Woodcock's boot that made the all-important connection to toe-poke the ball home. Woodcock claimed the goal, despite the feeling by some that Wolves player Derek Parkin had got the final touch. Who cared!

Shilton had to be on top form to keep out a Kenny Hibbitt thunderbolt from the narrowest of angles, catapulting his body backwards to palm the ball over. Just after, Hibbitt was played in by Richards, but screwed his shot inches off target. The only other item of note before the interval was a stunning twenty-yard shot from Robertson that skidded dangerously off the muddy surface. However, Wolves goalie Paul Bradshaw managed to pounce on the ball.

Wolves came out for the second half in a much more positive frame of mind. Geoff Palmer played the ball to Norman Bell, who headed it square for John Richards to whip in a swerving shot from long range that had Shilton scrambling across the line to keep the ball out from under his crossbar. The visitors had obviously decided upon a route-one strategy, whereas Forest and Robertson in particular, still favoured keeping the ball on the deck. On a couple of occasions, Robbo had to check to keep the ball under control. However, in the fifty-third minute, the brilliant winger launched in a beautifully flighted cross that eluded Wolves' defenders and into the run of John McGovern, and the ball hit the back of the net from his superb volley.

Those two moments of high drama brought Forest another two points as they extended their unbeaten run to eleven League games. Wolves didn't play all that badly, particularly Hibbitt and Carr who shone in midfield.

Aston Villa did Forest a favour by beating Arsenal 1-0 at Highbury, likewise Coventry with a 1-0 victory over Liverpool. Unfortunately Leicester couldn't spike Everton's guns, going down 2-0 at Goodison Park, and Leeds beat Ipswich 1-0.

Nottingham Forest 2
Woodcock (40), McGovern (53)

Wolverhampton Wanderers 0

Ian Bowyer.

The League table:

	PLD	W	D	L	F	A	PTS
Forest	**27**	**18**	**6**	**3**	**49**	**15**	**42**
Everton	27	14	8	5	52	31	36
Man City	26	15	4	7	59	27	34
Liverpool	27	14	6	7	35	20	34
Arsenal	27	14	5	8	35	22	33
Leeds	27	12	8	7	42	34	32

Elsewhere in the First Division, the following games were postponed: Derby v. Chelsea, Manchester United v. Manchester City, QPR v. West Ham, and West Brom v. Newcastle, plus many games in the other divisions. However, it was now back to League Cup action for Forest, where a bit of a daunting task lay ahead at Elland Road. Remember, Leeds United had been the last side to beat them.

Nottingham Forest: Shilton, Anderson, Barrett, McGovern, Needham, Burns, O'Neill, Gemmill, Withe, Woodcock, Robertson. Sub: Bowyer
Wolverhampton Wanderers: Bradshaw; Palmer, Parkin; Daley, Berry, McAlle; Hibbitt, Carr, Richards, Bell, Daly. Sub: Patching

LEEDS UNITED v. NOTTINGHAM FOREST

Football League Cup semi-final, first leg, Elland Road　　**Date:** Wednesday 8 February 1978
Attendance: 43,222　　　　　　　　　　　　　　　　　　　**Referee:** Mr C. White (Harrow)

Leeds had played some good stuff to reach the semi-finals of the League Cup, their games usually featuring a number of goals. A 3-0 win at Rochdale in the second round was followed by the 4-0 home thrashing of Colchester. Then a 3-1 victory away to Bolton in round four preceded their 4-1 demolition of high-flying Everton at Elland Road. Moreover, don't forget that Leeds had beaten Forest 1-0 in the League at Elland Road last November. Little wonder that the Leeds fans were feeling confident.

Cloughie had his continuing selection problems in this competition, again being without the services of the cup-tied Shilton, Gemmill and Needham. For this game, his problems were even more acute. In the end, he decided to play McGovern as stand-in central defender in the absence of Larry Lloyd, and to draft in John O'Hare. Naturally, in the time-honoured traditions of cup football, the barrel-chested striker scored against his old club.

Forest's depleted League Cup squad faced a pretty strong side at Elland Road on this bleak winter's evening, and didn't they do well? The Herculean defence, marshalled wonderfully by Kenny Burns, looked like they had been born to play together. All in all, Forest were hungrier for the ball, as well as being much faster to it, their overall play much more direct in its approach. In front of goal, they always looked likely to score.

Leeds were stunned by two goals from Peter Withe in as many minutes. First, in the nineteenth minute, he slammed the ball past David Harvey from close range, after racing in to meet Martin O'Neill's centre. Then, two minutes later, he dived bravely to head Tony Woodcock's cross wide of the Leeds 'keeper. Leeds weren't going to lie down and die, and hit back within seven minutes through Eddie Gray. The Scottish winger found space and scored with a fierce low shot in the twenty-eighth minute to bring the deficit back to one goal. The goal spurred Leeds on, but it's fair to say that despite a lot of possession and some excellent work in the middle of the park by Tony Currie, who was pushed back towards his own goal further and further as the game wore on, Leeds never really looked capable of upsetting Forest. Having been the last team to beat Forest, no doubt Leeds went into this game feeling that they could and should win it. However, this was an altogether different game to their previous encounter. Leeds' problems increased in the thirtieth minute, when Peter Lorimer, he of the rocket shot, was forced to limp off with a thigh injury to be replaced by Carl Harris. Forest were good value for their 2-1 lead at the break.

In the second half Leeds did managed to put together a sustained period of strong pressure, but, having said that, they hardly troubled Forest's eighteen-year-old 'keeper Chris Woods, or their makeshift defence. A third goal for Forest seemed inevitable, and sure enough it duly arrived. In the seventy-fifth minute, Forest had another little surprise for the home side, when they put together a beautiful six-man move that ended with John O'Hare restoring the Reds' two-goal advantage. Kenny

Leeds United 1	Nottingham Forest 3
Gray E. (28)	Withe 2 (19, 21),
	O'Hare (75)

Leeds United v. Nottingham Forest

John O'Hare, scorer against his old club.

Burns and O'Hare exchanged passes before sending Robertson away down the left. His pass found Withe who tried for goal, but the ball fell to O'Hare who stuck it past Harvey's right hand as neatly as you like. Leeds' only real reply came when Eddie Gray headed over the crossbar from a corner.

It was all over. Forest had won by three goals to one. A result that was a triumph for Brian Clough, who I am sure would have been rubbing his hands together with glee, having put one over on the club that had provided him with forty-four tempestuous days as manager at Elland Road. Trevor Cherry had earned a booking for scything down Viv Anderson, which just about summed up Leeds' dejection.

Leeds United v. Nottingham Forest

And now you're gonna believe us. The words of that football anthem were never so true, for now Forest were considered as serious contenders for the treble of home trophies. Six points clear in the League, almost certain of a League Cup place at Wembley, and still in the FA Cup. Who could stop them? It was difficult to see.

This fabulous win set up Forest for the second leg at the City Ground in a week's time. Surely only a miracle of Lazarus-type proportions could save Leeds. Their hopes of salvaging something from a disappointing season seemed to have all but disappeared.

Due to the 'big freeze', like many teams Forest had a Saturday off on 11 February 1978. Once again, the weather played havoc with outdoor sport as severe frost and snow caused widespread postponements and cancellations. All four race meetings in England and Ireland were cancelled, and the pools panel was called into action for the third successive Saturday. The postponed First Division games were: Aston Villa v. Nottingham Forest, Leeds United v. Derby County, Liverpool v. Ipswich Town, Middlesbrough v. Coventry City, Newcastle United v. Birmingham City, Norwich City v. Everton and Wolverhampton Wanderers v. West Bromwich Albion. Forest's game at Villa Park was one of the first games to be called off.

On 13 February Ally McLeod included Kenny Burns, Archie Gemmill and John Robertson in the Scotland squad to face Bulgaria on 22 February.

Forest's return League Cup game against Leeds scheduled for the 15 February was postponed for a week.

This was the week that a reporter sought retired football legend Bill Shankly's opinion as to whether Forest could hold on to win the League title. His reply was as passionate as ever: 'Ask yersel laddie. If they win their last seven home games, which with the exception of Leeds are all against teams from the bottom half of the table, they'll have 56 points. That's only one short of the total with which Liverpool won the title last season. If they win all their home games, and take in a few away points, they could be Champions without taking another point away from home, and something would have to go radically wrong for that to happen.' I think I know what he meant!

Leeds United: Harvey, Reaney, Gray F., Lorimer (Harris), Parkinson, Madeley, Cherry, Hankin, Currie, Gray E., Graham.
Nottingham Forest: Woods, Anderson, Barrett, McGovern, Burns, O'Hare, O'Neill, Bowyer, Withe, Woodcock, Robertson. Sub: Clark

QUEENS PARK RANGERS v. NOTTINGHAM FOREST

FA Cup fifth round, Loftus Road
Attendance: 26,803

Date: Saturday 18 February 1978
Referee: Mr K. Walmsley (Blackpool)

Forest's winning streak was halted temporarily at Loftus Road by a talented Rangers side, who found themselves locked in a relegation dogfight; a real top against bottom affair. With England's game against West Germany coming up on 22 February, manager Ron Greenwood came to cast an eye over Shilton and Needham; neither made the team.

The weather had not been kind, the icy playing surface threatening the staging of the game, until a large amount of sand was brought in to combat the conditions. In places, the heavily sanded pitch resembled the Sahara Desert. Forest took the game to Rangers, and ex-Walsall 'keeper Phil Parkes had to be alert to catch Robertson's free-kick under a heavy challenge from Burns. However the referee blew for a foul. Moments later, Ian Gillard put in an excellent challenge to snuff out the danger after Withe had cleverly flicked the ball into Rangers box. Withe and Woodcock were looking particularly dangerous, and only quick thinking by Parkes prevented a goalscoring opportunity. Then Barrett zipped in a centre that no one could reach.

Leighton James was allowed to carry the ball deep into the Forest half, before delivering a menacing centre that Burns reached before Busby, the Scot heading behind for a corner. Leighton James swung the ball over for Don Givens to head towards the corner of Forest's goal. Fortunately, Peter Withe was backing up and was able to steer the ball away. At this time, Rangers certainly had the upper hand. Forest's only effort was a snap shot from Archie Gemmill that Parkes smothered near his left-hand post, after Woodcock had played the Scot in. In their next attack, Rangers' mercurial frontman Stan Bowles was denied by John McGovern's block. Then John Hollins whipped in a wicked free-kick, but Burns again came to Forest's defence. However, in the eighteenth minute, QPR's dominance of possession brought them a goal. Stan Bowles' clever pass knifed through the Forest defence, and although Archie Gemmill slid in, he only succeeded in putting the ball behind. James' swerving corner looked like coming up short until in darted former Notts County striker Martyn Busby, whose near-post header beat a surprised Peter Shilton and flew into the net.

Forest redoubled their efforts to penetrate Rangers' defence, first Gemmill put Robertson away, but the linesman flagged for offside, and then Burns tried unsuccessfully to deceive Parkes with a viciously curling free-kick that missed the post by inches. Despite Forest's determination, Parkes could not be beaten. For Rangers, Givens and Busby were asking most of the questions, with the former Meadow Lane man getting into some worrying positions. From one effort, Needham managed to get Busby's shot back to Shilton. Then Bowles cleverly found James on the left. Two seconds later, the Welshman was on the floor where he had been unceremoniously dumped by Viv Anderson; a caution was the outcome. With the interval fast approaching, O'Neill combined brilliantly with McGovern and Gemmill to set up a shooting opportunity for Anderson, and only a top-class diving save prevented a certain goal for Forest. Then Parkes caught the resulting corner as the referee brought the half to a close.

Queens Park Rangers 1	Nottingham Forest 1
Busby (18)	O'Neill (89)

Queens Park Rangers v. Nottingham Forest

Rangers' instant attack might have caught out the Reds but for Gemmill's timely interception on Bowles' through ball. Then Burns was the saviour, taking the ball off James' toe as he was about to pull the trigger. The game quietened down for a while, with a series of mistakes resulting in a period of stalemate. Anderson put the ball behind for a corner on the left, and James' inswinger brought Shilton out of his goal to fist the ball to safety with Martyn Busby arrowing in at top speed. Soon after, Burns showed his pace when he beat Busby to a dangerous-looking through ball.

Forest returned fire, Burns almost reaching a free-kick from Robertson with his head. The ball came out to Withe who rifled a left-foot cracker just the wrong side of the post. Gillard needed treatment but was able to continue. Then Robertson took on the role of 'meat-in-the-sandwich' and fell headlong to the ground near the penalty spot. The Trent-enders, along with everyone except the most partisan Rangers supporter, shouted for a penalty, but unbelievably the referee waved play on.

A bad piece of misjudgement by Parkes allowed Woodcock to head the ball on to the head of Withe, but the Forest striker could only look on in anguish as Clement booted the ball off the line. Apart from a few breakouts, Rangers were now firmly penned in their own half, with Forest's besiegers pressing for the equaliser. Then finally, it came. The ball was swung over and there was Martin O'Neill to head the ball past Parkes.

In the only First Division League game on 18 February, Everton beat West Ham 2-1. The games between Manchester United and Leeds, plus Coventry versus Newcastle were postponed. A number of FA Cup games were also postponed. On the previous night Manchester City had drawn 2-2 at Bristol City in the League.

The League table:

	PLD	W	D	L	F	A	PTS
Forest	**27**	**18**	**6**	**3**	**49**	**15**	**42**
Everton	28	15	8	5	54	32	38
Man City	28	16	5	7	55	30	37
Liverpool	27	14	6	7	35	20	34
Arsenal	28	14	6	8	36	24	34
Leeds	27	12	8	7	42	34	32

England's 'B' team were in action in Augsburg on 21 February 1978 against West Germany. Dave Needham played in central defence in a 2-1 win.

The cup-ties were coming thick and fast for the Reds, next up was the home leg of the League Cup semi-final.

Nottingham Forest: Shilton, Anderson, Barrett, McGovern, Needham, Burns, O'Neill, Gemmill, Withe, Woodcock, Robertson. Sub: Bowyer

Queens Park Rangers: Parkes, Clement, Gillard, Hollins, Howe, Abbott, Shanks, Busby, James, Bowles, Givens. Sub: Cunningham

Nottingham Forest v. Leeds United

Football League Cup semi-final, second leg, City Ground   **Date:** Tuesday 22 February 1978
Attendance: 38,131   **Referee:** Mr C. Thomas (Treorchy)

After an early scare, the roof nearly came off at the City Ground when Forest walloped Leeds United 7-3 on aggregate, to cruise into the final of the 1978 Football League Cup. This win emphasised Forest's superiority over most League clubs, and certainly provided Liverpool, their opponents in the final at Wembley on 18 March, with a bit to think about.

Forest's 3-1 lead from the first leg was a nice cushion to take into this game, however, if anyone in Nottingham thought that Leeds would be easy to roll over, they were in for a rude awakening. Having said that, it was the Reds that went close first. John McGovern created an opening in the fifth minute for Ian Bowyer, but his left-foot shot smacked against the face of the crossbar with 'keeper Dave Stewart hopelessly beaten. Suddenly, in the thirteenth minute the 'lost cause' that Leeds were chasing looked to be achievable when they scored a cleverly worked goal. Eddie Gray moved down the left and found Allan Clarke with a sweet pass. The former England striker took the ball in his stride, before sliding it into the run of Frank Gray, whose stunning twenty-five-yard thunderbolt whizzed past Chris Woods to bring the aggregate score to 3-2. What would be Forest's response? Hold out for a draw? Not on your life! Within five minutes, they had equalised.

Ian Bowyer took a quick free-kick out to John Robertson, who whipped in a cross from deep on the left that was met at the far post by Martin O'Neill, and the slick move was finished off from close range by Peter Withe, to restore Forest's two-goal advantage. Less than a minute later, Arthur Graham pounced on a bit of slack play by Larry Lloyd to put Leeds back in front on the night. This goal brought the aggregate score to 4-3 in Forest's favour. That's how it stayed at the interval. Blimey! Bring on the Bovril, or something stronger!

Within five minutes of the restart, Cloughie's boys slid into top gear to grab the goal that took the sting out of Leeds. Robbo smashed over a low cross that Tony Woodcock, under pressure from United's defenders, did well to turn back to the waiting Bowyer, who made no mistake with a second equaliser of the night for the Reds. At an aggregate score of 5-3, it seemed unlikely that Leeds would be able to come back again. Three minutes later, following a Robertson corner, Larry Lloyd drilled the ball into the Leeds net, only for the goal to be chalked off by Clive Thomas, who ruled that he had pushed Stewart as he had gone for the ball. In the seventy-third minute, Martin O'Neill put Forest ahead for the first time in this game when he latched on to a long ball from Ian Bowyer, checked inside Paul Reaney, before beating Stewart to score a third for the Reds, to make it 3-2 on the night, 6-3 on aggregate.

All of a sudden, Leeds looked tired and dejected, and when Tony Woodcock collected a loose ball that had bounced off a defender following Robbo's cross, to run on and score a fourth, that just about finished them off. An aggregate score of 7-3 was indicative of Forest's approach to this game. A fabulous win, to be sure.

Nottingham Forest 4
  Withe (18), Bowyer (49),
  O'Neill (72), Woodcock (75)

Leeds United 2
  Gray F. (13), Graham (19)

NOTTINGHAM FOREST v. LEEDS UNITED

Viv Anderson takes on Leeds' Trevor Cherry.

Now Forest fans were beginning to get really excited about this season. Top of the League, already into the final of the League Cup, and hopefully soon into the quarter-finals of the FA Cup. And don't forget that they were unbeaten since 19 November 1977.

Cloughie had gone on holiday for one of the 'recharge-yer-battery-breaks' that he was so partial to.

Also on 22 February 1978, England lost an international friendly game 2-1 to West Germany in Munich, Stuart Pearson scoring for England. England: Clemence, Neal, Mills, Wilkins, Watson, Hughes (Capt.), Keegan (Francis), Coppell, Pearson, Brooking, Barnes.

Up north, Archie Gemmill helped Scotland beat Bulgaria 2-1 at Hampden Park.

Nottingham Forest: Woods, Anderson, Barrett, McGovern, Lloyd, Burns, O'Neill, Bowyer, Withe, Woodcock, Robertson. Sub: Clark

Leeds United: Stewart, Reaney, Hampton, Cherry, Gray F., Madeley, Gray E,, Hankin, Currie, Clarke, Graham. Sub: Parkinson

Norwich City v. Nottingham Forest

Football League First Division, Carrow Road
Attendance: 26,004

Date: Saturday 25 February 1978
Referee: Mr T.G. Bune (Billingshurst)

In a move calculated to blunt Forest's attacking flair, Norwich had Martin Peters starting off this game as sweeper, behind a back four. It was a tactic that obviously failed to work when Forest scored three goals in an eight-minute spell.

In the first significant attack, a high ball towards the Canaries' penalty area was suicidally back-headed by centre-back Jones into the run of Tony Woodcock. The young striker sped into the box, where goalkeeper Roger Hansbury came out to meet him and make an unbelievable save. The ball bounced clear off the 'keeper's knees. Forest continued to dominate the early stages of the game, and Barrett, the only outfield player in the team not to have scored so far this season, chased a hopeful pass but failed to get in the telling shot that would break his duck. At the Forest end, Keith Robson, making his first-team debut for Ken Brown's beleaguered side, found space, but put his shot well wide of the target. The Reds grabbed the opening goal in the sixteenth minute. McGuire upended Barrett as the full-back carried the ball forward. Archie Gemmill's lightning free-kick found Woodcock, who beat Powell with ease to reach the byline. The Norwich defenders moved to anticipate his cross, but he deceived them by rifling in a shot from the acutest of angles that deflected to Withe following up, giving the Forest number nine the easiest of chances to push the ball over the line; his fifth in the last six games, and his eighteenth of the season in all competitions.

Forest piled on the agony with a second goal six minutes after the first. Colin Barrett watched the dropping ball carefully, intent on volleying it at goal with his right foot. Unfortunately, his attempt failed to connect properly and the ball squirmed up off his boot to Gemmill, whose quick-thinking forward header was miskicked by Powell, amazingly dropping in front of Barrett. This time, the young full-back met the ball cleanly with an explosive shot that flew past Hansbury. His teammates swarmed around an ecstatic Barrett, whose beaming smile flashed around Carrow Road.

As if to rub it in, Forest made it three two minutes later. On twenty-four minutes, Martin O'Neill received the ball just inside the Norwich half, and set off on a mazy run that the Canaries seemed powerless to stop. Moving into the penalty area, he unleashed a beautiful left-foot shot in the corner of the net. Now it looked like only a question of how many Forest would get, as the home side had no answer to Forest's power. The faithful were singing, 'We're going to win the treble.'

Did the Reds unwittingly drop down a few gears? Who knows. All that counted was that they now contrived to throw away a three-goal lead in a game that they should have won at a canter. Totally against the run of play, Forest allowed a demoralised Norwich back into the game. First McGuire fired in a stinging twenty-five-yarder that Shilton caught faultlessly. Then Needham missed a fairly simple header, the ball sliding into the danger area off his head. Fortunately, Burns

Norwich City 3
Ryan (penalty 44),
Suggett (68), Robson (70)

Nottingham Forest 3
Withe (16), Barrett (22),
O'Neill (24)

was on hand to tidy up. Seconds later, a corner from Paddon almost reached the head of Gibbins, but Forest managed to get the ball away. Paddon's next cross gave Norwich a glimmer of hope. Seconds into injury time, Peters challenged Barrett in the air, and the Forest left-back handled the ball. Up stepped John Ryan to strike his penalty wide of Shilton. Half-time: Norwich 1, Forest 3.

Forest emerged from the tunnel determined to grab a fourth goal. Woodcock was floored by Peters on the edge of the box, but the free-kick was wasted. O'Neill shot wide under pressure from Powell, then Gemmill flicked on McGovern's pass to Woodcock, but again a good situation was wasted when he fired wide. Peters let in Withe, who set up O'Neill with a neat touch; however, the Irishman lifted his effort the wrong side of the top corner. It was all Forest, but chance after chance went begging. Next, it was Hansbury diving to keep out Woodcock's effort that kept the score at 3-1. Forest were denied a bolt-on penalty, when McGuire scythed down Archie Gemmill in the box. The frustration was obvious, but surely, another goal would come sooner than later. It did, but at the wrong end.

Norwich struck twice in two minutes to bring an amazing turnaround to the scoreline. First Peters headed down a centre from Colin Sullivan that Colin Suggett reached first to poke the ball into the net. Unbelievable! Shilton hadn't conceded more than one goal in a competitive match since joining from Stoke in September 1977. Suddenly, the Canaries were all over Forest like a rash. The Reds put up the shutters, or so they believed. Norwich won the ball from the restart and stormed onto the attack. Forest's defenders managed to block two shots, the last of which dropped invitingly for debutant Keith Robson, who smashed the ball past Shilton. Three-all! The Norwich fans went crazy, and their team sensed blood. With a full twenty minutes left on the ref's watch, it was backs-to-the-wall stuff for the Reds from now until the final whistle.

Suggett found himself in acres of space, and missed an absolute sitter, ballooning his shot way over the bar from only a few yards out. Then a Suggett free-kick reached Paddon, who snatched his left-foot shot behind. Despite being under the cosh for the next ten minutes or so, Forest doggedly defended the point that they so nearly threw away. The relief on their faces when the referee blew for time was evident for all to see. Cloughie would not be best pleased when his lieutenants reported what had happened.

A mixed bag of results for the chasing pack: West Bromwich Albion 3 Coventry 3, West Ham 2 Arsenal 2, Birmingham 1 Villa 0, Leeds 2 Chelsea 0, Liverpool 3 Manchester United 1, Manchester City 1 Everton 0. Forest were still flying high, 4 points clear with a game in hand.

The League table:

	PLD	W	D	L	F	A	PTS
Forest	**28**	**18**	**7**	**3**	**52**	**18**	**43**
Man City	29	17	5	7	56	30	39
Everton	29	15	8	6	54	33	38
Liverpool	28	15	6	7	38	21	36
Arsenal	29	14	7	8	38	26	35
Leeds	28	13	8	7	44	34	34

NORWICH CITY v. NOTTINGHAM FOREST

England World Cup winner Martin Peters.

John McGovern was doubtful for Forest's next game as he had picked up a groin strain at Norwich, and Colin Barrett had injured his ankle in the same match.

Norwich City: Hansbury, Ryan, Sullivan, McGuire, Jones, Powell, Robson K., Paddon, Gibbins, Suggett, Peters. Sub: Bond K.

Nottingham Forest: Shilton, Anderson, Barrett, McGovern, Needham, Burns, O'Neill, Gemmill, Withe, Woodcock, Robertson. Sub: Bowyer

Nottingham Forest v. Queens Park Rangers

FA Cup fifth round replay, City Ground
Attendance: 40,097

Date: Monday 27 February 1978
Referee: Mr K. Walmsley (Thornton, Blackpool)

A second stalemate in this round of the cup, Forest's second consecutive draw, their third in four games. Thank goodness for the trusty boot of Robbo. Dave Needham took McGovern's position, and the reliable Frank Clark came in for Barrett. Archie Gemmill was also forced to miss this one, Ian Bowyer replacing him. Forest pushed Kenny Burns into midfield with Larry Lloyd coming in at the back.

One of the main talking points of this FA Cup fifth-round replay came in the second minute of extra time, when Rangers' former England defender, Dave Clement stripped off his shirt and threw it to the ground in disgust after being sent off by referee Ken Walmsley, leaving his depleted teammates to hang on to earn a fighting draw at the City Ground, and thus live to fight again another day. Clement had been booked in the fifty-ninth minute, along with Peter Withe, after the pair had clashed angrily. The QPR defender was shown the red card after scything down John Robertson, who had obviously gone past him once too often.

Clement would most likely be charged with bringing the game into disrepute following his disgraceful display of petulance. His action could cost him very dearly. Four years earlier, Leeds United's Billy Bremner and Liverpool's Kevin Keegan received a one month ban and were each fined £500 after a similar display of temper-fuelled striptease at Wembley in the 1974 Charity Shield. The Rangers' full-back might well have gone after seventy-four minutes of the game when he unceremoniously chopped down Forest's stand-in captain Kenny Burns. However, for some strange reason the referee chose to turn a blind eye to what was a disgusting piece of foul play. His overdue dismissal was probably the climax to this bruising, but otherwise exciting cup tie.

Forest came at Rangers in determined fashion, intent on brushing their opponents aside, and it's fair to say that they pretty much achieved their objective, save for one tiny detail, namely when QPR equalised. Early on, Phil Parkes looked well beaten by a beautiful shot from Tony Woodcock that somehow, future bad boy Clement cleared off the line. Then Ian Bowyer took the ball round Parkes before clipping in what should have been a certain goal, but which Howe reached to head off the line from under his crossbar. Not long after this, Woodcock's glorious glancing header rebounded off the inside of a post straight into the arms of a relieved Phil Parkes. It was all Forest, and their sensational attacking display finally earned a deserved breakthrough, when they went ahead from a penalty after nineteen minutes. Woodcock played a glorious ball to Robertson in the QPR box, and Forest's number eleven neatly sidestepped a strong challenge from Clement, before eventually being tripped by Ian Gillard. Robbo got to his feet and placed the ball on the spot, before sending his spot kick to the right, well out of Parkes' reach.

This should have been the signal for Forest to cruise on into a sixth-round trip to West Bromwich Albion. Instead, they were robbed of a victory when Rangers surprised them with an equaliser two

Score after extra time:

Nottingham Forest 1
Robertson (penalty 19)

Queens Park Rangers 1
Shanks (43)

NOTTINGHAM FOREST v. QUEENS PARK RANGERS

Martin O'Neill in action against QPR.

minutes before half-time. Leighton James took the ball down the left, before whipping over his cross, which Martyn Busby headed down into the danger area. First to the ball was Don Shanks who just about managed to scramble a shot past Peter Shilton. That was to be the last contribution to the Rangers cause by Welsh winger James, who suffered a reoccurrence of a knee injury, his place being taken after the break by substitute Paul McGee.

The story of the second half was a little different. The impetus of the goal, coupled with the introduction of the fresh legs of McGee seemed to put a bit more gas in the QPR tank. The youngster displayed plenty of enthusiasm and effort to spur on his comrades, and in a complete reversal, Rangers gradually took charge of the game. Their best attempt came from Busby who slammed a great header against the bar. At the other end, Phil Parkes also had to be at his very best to keep out two well-struck shots by Robertson.

Thirty minutes of extra time did nothing to change the scoreline. In fact, after the sending off of Clements, Rangers shut-up shop, concentrating on holding onto the draw. This was one of those gruelling cup ties in which several other players might have been dismissed. The referee also took the names of Howe in the twentieth minute and Abbott in the thirty-sixth minute. Another game in an already congested fixture list was something that Brian Clough did not welcome.

Nottingham Forest v. Queens Park Rangers

QPR manager Frank Sibley was clearly not a happy bunny with the decision of the FA that the second replay of this unresolved tie must take place only three days after such an exhausting game. 'It's unfair, because we had been asked to postpone the original replay for Forest's benefit, so that players involved in England matches would be free.'

Cloughie returned to the UK from a family holiday in Majorca for the second replay, then went back to the sunshine after his team had won.

Peter Shilton MBE, CBE was an outstanding, world-class goalkeeper. He joined Forest from Stoke City for a fee of £270,000 in September 1977. For the Potters he made 110 League appearances. Shilton made his debut for Forest in the 2-0 defeat of Aston Villa at the City Ground on 17 September 1977, going on to make 202 League appearances for the Reds. The PFA's 1978 Player of the Year was undoubtedly one of the best goalkeepers ever to pull on a jersey. Shilton was also honoured with the PFA Merit Award in 1990.

A member of Forest's two successful European Cup-winning teams, Peter was born in Leicester on 18 September 1949, joining his home town team as an apprentice in September 1966, where he made 286 League appearances, including one in the Foxes' losing cup final team in 1969, scoring, yes, scoring 1 goal, before transferring to Stoke City for £325,000.

Between his England debut against East Germany on 25 November 1970 and his last game in July 1990, he won a record 125 caps for an England goalkeeper. It would surely have been many more had 61 cap-winning Ray Clemence not been around at the same time. Shilts played for England in the finals of three World Cups and two European Championships. Added to the above are 3 Under-23 caps, plus a number for the England youth side.

On the domestic side, Peter had a much-travelled career, moving to Southampton from Forest for £300,000 in August 1982, where he made 188 League appearances. He then transferred to Derby County in July 1987 for £90,000, turning out in 175 League games for the Rams. Shilton then had a spell at Plymouth Argyle as player-manager from March 1992 until December 1994, making 34 appearances in the League. Then he was a non-contract player with Wimbledon, without making an appearance, and then went to Bolton Wanderers, making 1 substitute appearance, before moving as goalkeeping cover to Coventry in July 1995, West Ham in January 1996 (no appearances for either club) and finally joining Leyton Orient in November 1996, where he played 9 times. A short spell at Middlesbrough heralded the end of a long and illustrious career, and Peter finally hung up his gloves. While at Orient, Peter made his record-breaking 1,000 League appearance, the first, and to date the only player in the history of the game to reach this milestone. This televised game was Orient against Brighton in December 1996. In all, including 125 internationals, Shilts played in 1,375 senior games, making 1,005 League appearances.

Nottingham Forest: Shilton, Anderson, Clark, Needham, Lloyd, Burns, O'Neill, Bowyer, Withe, Woodcock, Robertson. Sub: O'Hare

Queens Park Rangers: Parkes, Clement, Gillard, Hollins, Howe, Abbott, Shanks, Busby, James (McGee), Bowles, Givens.

Nottingham Forest v. Queens Park Rangers

FA Cup fifth round, second replay, City Ground   **Date:** Thursday 2 March 1978
Attendance: 33,960   **Referee:** Mr G. Courtney (Spennymoor)

After 300 minutes of football, this tie finally had a winner. Fortunately, it was Forest. The game was a gruelling, hard-fought mud-splattered encounter, and though it may have lacked a little of the drama of their previous encounter, it certainly was a thriller.

Forest's first attack almost produced a goal inside sixty seconds. Anderson stretched his long legs on one of his typical marauding runs that saw him penetrate deep into the Rangers box to beat Phil Parkes in a challenge for the ball, which now ran loose towards Peter Withe who couldn't quite fasten on to it. Seconds later, it was Anderson again scything through the QPR defence to set up a chance for Withe, but again no goal resulted from his effort. Then in the second minute Forest's fantastic attacking start delivered the goal that they had threatened to score.

Robertson sent Woodcock on a run that took him to the byline, from where he smashed in a low hard cross that spun off Parkes under challenge from Withe to the far post where Martin O'Neill was haring in to execute the simple task of poking the ball home. Gosh! What a start.

It took around five minutes of treatment to a nasty facial injury before the Rangers 'keeper Phil Parkes could resume. Now Parkes became an even bigger hero for Rangers as he almost single-handedly defied Forest's blistering attack. Martin O'Neill sent Anderson galloping down the right to get in a dangerous cross that Withe met first time, forcing a great diving save from Parkes as he pushed the ball away from danger. Forest built again; this time Frank Clark combined well with Robbo, who fed the ball to Ian Bowyer, before the midfielder cleverly laid the ball to Tony Woodcock, who thumped in a fierce drive that Parkes saved athletically. QPR breathed a sigh of relief as momentarily at least they managed to take the game to Forest. A neat piece of interplay ended with Tommy Cunningham cracking in a tremendous shot that had Peter Shilton flying across his goal to push the ball away. Then a mix-up in the Reds' defence presented a shooting chance for Paul McGee. However, the young Irish striker fired his effort straight at Shilton.

Forest almost extended their lead a couple of times before the interval. First Robbo smashed in a low drive that Parkes smothered at the foot of a post, seconds before Peter Withe missed the best chance of the match. Racing onto a lovely through ball from Tony Woodcock, the Forest number nine looked a certainty to score, but with only Phil Parkes to beat, Withe somehow contrived to spoon his shot over the crossbar. Half-time: 1-0 to Forest.

Within a few minutes of the start of the second half, referee George Courtney had booked Tommy Cunningham for bringing down Kenny Burns, and Larry Lloyd for whipping Paul McGee's legs from under him. And now Rangers suddenly seemed to remember that they too could play thoughtful attacking football. Former County striker Martyn Busby, back at the club that had originally let him go, forced his way into the box, only to be denied by Shilton who dived bravely at his feet. And minutes later, had to go full length to keep out a corner from Stan Bowles that deflected off Martin

---

Nottingham Forest 3   **Queens Park Rangers 1**
   O'Neill (2), Woodcock 2 (65,79)   Bowles (64)

Nottingham Forest v. Queens Park Rangers

O'Neill. Four minutes after the hour mark, Rangers' spell of pressure paid off with the equaliser. Frank Clark looked to have the ball under control when he allowed Stan Bowles to jostle the ball away from him. However, the Rangers wizard still had a lot to do, but he did it, and did it well. Brilliantly wrong-footing Shilton, Bowles slid the ball home from a tight angle.

Rangers' joy quickly turned to tears when a minute later Forest grabbed the lead back. Kenny Burns found Woodcock with a long raking pass and the Forest striker did the rest with a tremendous shot that flew past Parkes. QPR hit back with a Bowles free-kick that Shilton was forced to fist clear, and then thankfully, Dave Needham managed to fling himself in front of McGee's shot that looked like it was heading for goal. With eleven minutes to go Forest scored the all-important third goal.

As if to make amends for his earlier error, Frank Clark hit a long ball over Withe's shoulder for the big striker to run on to. Unfortunately, Ron Abbott raced across to reach the ball first, but unluckily for Ron, his attempted back-pass to Parkes stuck fast in the City Ground mud only feet from where Tony Woodcock was waiting. The young England striker swooped onto the ball, taking it round the Rangers 'keeper to slot it into the net. Surely, that would kill off Rangers. But no, all it did was to fire up a spirited fightback from the West Londoners. Stan Bowles whipped in a fierce cross-shot that struck a Forest defender before bouncing clear, then Busby repeated the move, with the same end result.

Referee Courtney blew his whistle to signal the end of this epic saga. Forest had won, and won well. However, Rangers had their moments and shouldn't feel too aggrieved, they had played their part in a thrilling encounter, and could hold their heads up high. Maybe their performance against the League leaders would provide the stimulus in their fight against relegation. For Forest, the 'impossible' treble was still well and truly on.

An interesting bit of news was reported on 3 March. It appeared that Frank Sinatra had signed for Third Division Port Vale. The report turned out to be a bit of an exaggeration to say the least. Apparently, the struggling club had written to the star crooner in Las Vegas, sending him a brand-new one-dollar bill, which they discovered was reputed to bring the recipient good luck. Frank signed it and sent it back. Vale hoped it would work. (Postscript: Maybe it did, because at the end of the season Vale finished fourth from bottom, thus avoiding relegation).

The bad news for the Reds was that Viv Anderson had picked up a two-match ban.

Nottingham Forest: Shilton, Anderson, Clark, Needham, Lloyd, Burns, O'Neill, Bowyer, Withe, Woodcock, Robertson. Sub: O'Hare

Queens Park Rangers: Parkes, Cunningham, Gillard, Hollins, Howe, Abbott, Shanks, Busby, McGee (Williams), Bowles, Givens.

Nottingham Forest v. West Ham United

Football League First Division, City Ground
Attendance: 33,924

Date: Saturday 4 March 1978
Referee: Mr K. Hackett (Sheffield)

Forest took their third point off the Hammers with a bit of a patched-up defensive line-up. This was the first time that Clough had been forced to make wholesale changes. Those two Mr Versatiles, Messrs Bowyer and O'Hare, came in as replacements for Viv Anderson, missing his first game of the season through suspension, and John McGovern. Dave Needham moved to the heart of the defence in place of Larry Lloyd. Frank Clark continued at left-back. There was no need to worry because everyone slotted into their positions as smooth as silk. West Ham were languishing perilously close to the foot of the table. However, it took the Reds quite a time to break down their dogged defence.

Forest began slowly, and it was West Ham that were first to put together an attack, but in each case, the Reds' defence moved forward as one to catch former Rams striker Derek Hales offside. A bit surprising was the Hammers' use of the long ball, especially considering the artistry of Brooking, Curbishley and Devonshire, It seemed that they weren't interested in playing the slick brand of pure football that West Ham teams had become known for. Having said that, on a few occasions they did revert to their 'old style' and managed to carve out a couple of excellent chances, the best of which resulted in Derek Hales' unbelievable miss when presented with an open goal.

Alan Devonshire latched on to a loose ball and surprised Forest with the speed of his run. With his defenders out of position, Shilton had no choice but to come out of his goal to narrow the angle. Now Devonshire tricked the Forest goalkeeper by laying the ball back to the inrushing Hales, who had managed to get free of his marker. But with an open goal to shoot at, somehow, and quite incredibly, the West Ham striker whipped his shot wide of the post.

This miraculous escape stung the Reds into action, and they now moved onto the attack with some venom. There followed an amazing sequence of events that saw Bobby Ferguson and the visitors' goal somehow survive everything Forest threw at them. Surely, the Hammers wouldn't be able to keep a clean sheet up to the interval, but they did, stubbornly refusing to allow Forest to roll them over as they had done in the League Cup in August. Half-time: 0-0.

The second half opened with Forest striving for the breakthrough, which just wouldn't come. Ferguson and his defenders were putting in a gritty defensive performance, with a couple of over exuberant tackles producing bookings. Then with just over ten minutes to go, Forest finally got that all-important first goal. Alan Curbishley stupidly earned himself a booking for dissent. Ian Bowyer took the free-kick, curling the ball into the visitors' box towards a host of players. First to the ball was Dave Needham, whose well-directed downward header bounced under Ferguson's dive and into the net. A few West Ham heads went down and within two minutes Forest grabbed a second, albeit with a slight element of good fortune.

The Hammers failed to clear the ball, which was then knocked back into the penalty area. The barrel chest of John O'Hare was used to good purpose, guiding the cross towards goal, where Frank

Nottingham Forest 2	West Ham United 0
Needham (79),	
Robertson (penalty 81)	

NOTTINGHAM FOREST v. WEST HAM UNITED

Lampard (senior) rashly stuck out his arm to block the ball. Penalty! An absolutely clear-cut penalty. All the Forest fans knew it would be 2-0 even before Robbo placed the ball on the spot, but horror of horrors, Ferguson guessed correctly and dived to stop Robbo's well-struck shot just inside the post. Hands were wrapped around heads in disbelief. Forest's ace penalty taker had missed. But hang on a minute; the referee is blowing his whistle, pointing to Ferguson and then the penalty spot, ordering the kick to be retaken because the Hammers' goalie had moved before the kick had been taken. A relieved Robertson placed the ball on the whitewashed spot again, and this time, whacked the ball high into the roof of the net, giving Ferguson no chance. That must have taken some bottle.

Well, that was just about it, West Ham were beaten, and probably feeling very demoralised. The final whistle was a blessed relief from the drama of that last ten or so minutes. Phew!

Great news for Forest fans: Manchester City had lost to Arsenal, and Chelsea had beaten Liverpool 3-1. However, the Scousers' manager Bob Paisley refused to concede the title.

Scotland manager Ally MacLeod announced his initial squad of forty players for the 1978 World Cup finals, and yes, the list included Kenny Burns, Archie Gemmill and John Robertson.

On the evening of 8 March, England's Under-21 side beat Italy at Maine Road, with Tony Woodcock scoring twice. In another Under-21 game, Martin O'Neill played for Northern Ireland in a 1-1 draw with Eire.

Also on 8 March, as expected, Dave Clement of QPR was officially charged with bringing the game into disrepute following his tantrum and sending off at the City Ground.

The games were still coming thick and fast; the more successful you are, the more congested your fixture list. Next up, a mouth-watering quarter-final against the Baggies.

Frank Clark was born in Highfield on 9 September 1943, playing first for Crook Town before joining his local club Newcastle United, where he helped win the forerunner of the UEFA Cup, the Inter Cities Fairs Cup in 1969. After 389 League appearances for the Magpies, Clough signed him on a free transfer in February 1975, and he made his debut against Plymouth Argyle on 16 August 1975, going on to make 155 first-team appearances in a Forest shirt, scoring 1 goal. He was an ever-present in seasons 1975/76 and 1976/77. After being released in May 1981, he accepted the position of assistant manager of Sunderland, and subsequently became manager of Orient. In May 1993, Frank Clark followed the legendary Brian Clough as manager of Forest. He also managed Manchester City.

Nottingham Forest: Shilton, Bowyer, Clark. O'Hare, Needham, Burns, O'Neill, Gemmill, Withe, Woodcock, Robertson. Sub: Lloyd

West Ham United: Ferguson; McDowell, Lampard, Curbishley, Taylor, Green, Devonshire, Robson B., Cross, Brooking, Hales. Sub: Holland

West Bromwich Albion v. Nottingham Forest

FA Cup quarter-final, The Hawthorns
Attendance: 36,506

Date: Saturday 11 March 1978
Referee: Mr P. Partridge (County Durham)

Oh well! I guess the bubble had to burst at some point. The Albion comfortably beat a poor Forest side, some of whom most probably, and understandably, had one eye on the League Cup final in six days time. This defeat ended Forest's fantastic sequence of twenty-two games unbeaten, and dreams of the magical treble. Peter Taylor missed this one; he was on holiday in Majorca, where I am sure the sangria would have tasted a bit sour when he found out that Forest had lost.

Ron Atkinson's West Brom side had a lot of class, earning a growing reputation for playing what the press vicariously described as 'sexy football.' John McGovern made the starting line-up for the first time since the Norwich game on 25 February; however, he was really only about half-fit. Viv Anderson was still suspended, Colin Barrett and Larry Lloyd injured. Albion would be without future England captain Bryan Robson. However, with Paddy Mulligan, Derek Statham, Cyrille Regis and Ally Brown all recovering from injuries, Albion were almost at full strength. Atkinson had taken over in January, inheriting a team from Ronnie Allen that was already earning rave reviews; he was wise enough not to mess about with it too much; a solid defence, a skilful midfield, and the find of the season leading the attack.

Forest and Albion came out of the traps like a couple of express trains, moving the ball around skilfully and with lightning pace, with the Reds marginally looking favourite to score first. Ian Bowyer's excellent pass was whipped over by Woodcock, but Mulligan was able to head the ball out of play. Clark then fed Robertson's kick into the area; however, the ball was much too high for Kenny Burns and Albion were able to clear the danger.

Albion's ability hadn't resulted in too much penetration thus far. In fact, their only attempt on goal was a speculative long-range effort from Mulligan that Shilton caught with ease. Then Albion got through to win a corner. Shilton and Ally Brown went up for Johnson's centre, which the Forest 'keeper dropped at the feet of John Wile, who lifted the ball high into the terraces. It didn't matter, because Pat Partridge had already blown his whistle, judging that Brown had impeded Shilton. Trewick took a blow to the head that held up play while he had treatment, and then Clark needed to be quick to clear Wile's header from a Johnson cross. Minute's later, Martin O'Neill sent in a powerful header that Godden turned around the post.

This first-class save from Tony Godden seemed to give the home side an extra lift, bringing more urgency to Albion's game, with Willie Johnson in particular, who by the way, had worn a tartan hat when the players ran onto the pitch, now displaying his speed and undoubted skills. As the quarter-hour approached, the Scottish winger was brought down on the left. The resultant free-kick from Statham somehow found its way past the group of players at the near post to drop invitingly into the middle of the box. Instinctively Irish international Mick Martin stuck out his foot and made contact. Unhappily, for Forest, the ball flew up into the air to loop over the head of Peter Shilton and into the

---

West Bromwich Albion 2
Martin (15), Regis (47)

Nottingham Forest 0

WEST BROMWICH ALBION v. NOTTINGHAM FOREST

Albion's Ally Brown beats Frank Clark to the ball.

corner of the Forest net. This was one of those lucky goals that Martin probably couldn't have repeated if he had stayed there for the rest of his life. Martin undoubtedly claimed that he had deliberately lobbed the ball over Shilton.

Then an error by Burns almost let in Albion for a second. The former Blues player mistakenly allowed a Johnson centre to get past him. The ball ran to a surprised-looking Ally Brown, who hurriedly prodded wide of Shilton's post. Martin O'Neill was the pick of the Forest forwards, regularly turning young Derek Statham first one way and then the other. Unfortunately, none of his excellent work brought a goal. For the remainder of the half, both sides probed for an opening, with Johnson's trickery being matched by John Robertson. With the World Cup coming up in the summer, both wingers were being watched by Scottish international manager Ally MacLeod.

For a long period after the goal, all-action Forest were in control, without managing to make the breakthrough that their dominance deserved. Even so, it's probably fair to say that at either end of the park, the defenders were in command. Whatever type of ball was pumped into the box, John Wile and Ally Robertson for Albion and Needham and Burns for Forest were equal to the task. Both sets of central defenders were backed up by the competent goalkeeping of Tony Godden and Peter Shilton. Albion led 1-0 at the interval.

After the break, the Baggies again came out fastest, catching Forest cold to take a two-goal lead. Two minutes after the restart, big Cyrille Regis notched his sixth goal in four games to win it for the Baggies, and put them into their eighteenth FA Cup semi-final. Albion's attackers stretched out the

WEST BROMWICH ALBION v. NOTTINGHAM FOREST

Forest defence across the full width of the pitch, creating large gaps, one of which Regis exploited, taking the ball into the Forest area before unleashing his accurate shot into the corner of the net.

Forest knew they had to do something, and came back strongly with a number of good attempts on goal. An Ian Bowyer free-kick looked likely to provide the opportunity to reduce the deficit. The ball curled into the box for Dave Needham to turn cleverly, but unfortunately, his rising right-foot shot skimmed the angle of post and bar. Then in an incisive attack that might have led to a Forest goal, O'Neill beat Statham again. This time, the Irishman slipped the ball inside to John Robertson. Sadly, he wasn't able to control it and the ball ran free. Lady Luck was momentarily wearing red, as Peter Withe was first to the ball. Forest's number nine looked up and thumped in a first-time screamer that on another day might have gone in. This time it didn't and Forest were beaten. Big Ron named Ally Brown as his man of the match.

The other FA Cup results were: Wrexham 2 Arsenal 3; Middlesbrough 0 Orient 0; Millwall 1 Ipswich 6.

In the League, Everton won 1-0 at Bristol City, Liverpool beat Leeds 1-0, and Coventry beat Leicester 1-0. Forest were 4 points in front with two games in hand.

	PLD	W	D	L	F	A	PTS
Forest	**29**	**19**	**7**	**3**	**54**	**18**	**45**
Everton	31	16	9	6	58	36	41
Man City	30	17	5	8	56	33	39
Arsenal	31	15	8	8	41	26	38
Liverpool	31	16	6	9	42	28	38
Coventry	30	15	7	8	58	46	37

Peter Withe was summoned to an FA disciplinary committee meeting in Manchester after amassing twenty penalty points. His previously good record (he had been booked only nine times in eight seasons) was taken into account. The Committee decided to be lenient and he was banned for one game starting from the following Monday.

On 9 March, Blackpool's Paul Hart signed for Leeds United for a fee of £300,000.

Now it was back to League action for a local derby that Forest just had to win. A little pride needed restoring. John McGovern was still suffering from a groin strain, and Colin Barrett's ankle injury hadn't cleared up, so both were considered doubtful for the game against the Foxes.

West Bromwich Albion: Godden, Mulligan, Statham, Tony Brown, Wile, Robertson, Martin, Ally Brown, Regis, Trewick, Johnston. Sub: Cunningham

Nottingham Forest: Shilton, Bowyer, Clark, McGovern, Needham, Burns, O'Neill, Gemmill, Withe, Woodcock, Robertson. Sub: O'Hare

Nottingham Forest v. Leicester City

Football League First Division, City Ground
Attendance: 32,355

Date: Tuesday 14 March 1978
Referee: Mr A.W. Grey (Great Yarmouth)

Forest quickly got over their FA Cup disappointment by completing the double over rivals Leicester courtesy of a John Robertson penalty, in the process getting them back on track for the League title.

Viv Anderson returned to the line-up in his usual right-back spot, John O'Hare continued in the number four shirt, with Ian Bowyer in Peter Withe's number nine jersey; the big striker was serving his one-match ban. This was one of those games where the top teams don't play particularly well, but still manage to grind out a result. Having said that, there were times when the Reds almost reached the devastating form that had so demoralised some of the best teams in the division. Make no mistake; Leicester knew they had been in a game, and that they had been lucky to meet Forest on a night when their near-neighbours didn't feel the need to take their opponents apart. Mind you, the wind that gusted and swirled around the City Ground didn't make for a night of pretty football.

It was fairly easy to see why Leicester were cemented to the foot of the table, so maybe Forest recognised that they were a bit of a pushover. Were they complacent? Well, as most football pundits know, there is no place for complacency at whatever level you are playing. Any game can be lost, for as we have heard so often, it only takes a second to score a goal. In the thirteenth minute, one of those 'seconds' came Forest's way. Frank Clark slid the ball into the Foxes penalty area for Ian Bowyer to run on to. Across came Steve Sims, who stuck out a leg, and according to referee Alf Grey, caught the Forest player's ankle for a clear penalty Every stout-hearted Red thought so, and so did the ref. Leicester's players and travelling fans disagreed. Undeterred by all the fuss, Robbo grabbed the ball, placed it on the spot, and smacked the ball to Mark Wallington's left.

Robbo's penalty brought fresh life to Forest's play, and at the same time, visibly took its toll on the Foxes, who for a time looked a demoralised bunch. On twenty-one minutes, big John O'Hare brought a magnificent save from Wallington. Archie Gemmill's probing run took him to the edge of the box, and when the ball came to O'Hare, he turned and shot in one movement to bring a brilliant save from the Leicester 'keeper. Then Forest were presented with a chance by full-back Steve Whitworth, who carelessly played the ball to Martin O'Neill. In turn, the Irishman found Woodcock, who took the ball to the byline, before sending in a low cross that Dennis Rofe almost turned into his own net.

Forest continued to launch attacks against the struggling Leicester defence, but couldn't find the extra spark needed to open them up. It wasn't that they were playing badly, just that there was something lacking. Maybe those pre-Wembley nerves were getting into the players' subconscious, or perhaps it was sheer exhaustion from playing so many important games in such a short time. Whatever it was, the fans hoped that Cloughie could sort it out at half-time. As it was, the rest of the first forty-five minutes passed without much incident. Half-time: 1-0 to Forest.

Nottingham Forest 1
Robertson (penalty 13)

Leicester City 0

Nottingham Forest v. Leicester City

Thou shalt not pass! Peter Shilton in determined mood.

For the second half, Leicester brought on Roger Davies for the injured Steve Sims, the ex-Rams striker having cost the Foxes a reported £160,000 from Belgian outfit Bruges. The break over, Forest got down to business, and within two minutes Martin O'Neill played in Archie Gemmill, who carried the ball forward and then blasted a screamer just past the angle of post and bar. This sparked Leicester into life, maybe they decided that with a bit more dash, they might take advantage of Forest's 'off' night. After a good move, Geoff Salmons whipped in a speculative left-foot shot that went narrowly wide. Then Leicester should have equalised when young Geordie Trevor Christie completely missed his kick in front of goal when he really should have buried the chance. Shortly after this, Roger Davies burst through the Forest defence and only Shilton's timely and brave dive at the striker's feet prevented a goal.

Time for Forest to wake up, and for a while, they did. Robbo worked his way down the left and found Ian Bowyer with a neat pass that Forest's flame-haired utility man leathered left-footed with all his might. Wallington, surprised by the power of the shot, could only parry the ball, which flew upwards off the 'keeper's hands, and he was able to collect it at the second attempt.

In the seventy-fifth minute, Keith Weller started and finished the best move of the match. The former England player played a fabulous ball into the path of the overlapping Whitworth, before running into space to take the return and cracking in a powerful rising drive with his right-foot. The ball beat Peter Shilton's leap all ends up, but to Weller's horror, he watched his effort skim the outside of the post.

The move had Cloughie leaping from the dugout to berate his players, and tell them that they needed to concentrate. Forest certainly needed another goal, and they almost got it within three minutes. O'Hare swapped passes with Robbo, before the latter sent in a tasty-looking cross that Woodcock met with a beautifully timed run, rifling in a low shot that Wallington did well to keep out. Fortunately, Forest managed to hang onto their lead for the final few minutes, and no doubt welcomed the sound of Alf Grey's whistle a lot more than the Foxes.

In a game dominated to some extent by the swirling wind, Leicester gave the ball away with far too much regularity, a trait that they would need to fix rapidly if they were to have any chance of staying out of the Second Division. That they held Forest to one goal, and that a penalty, was more down to the Reds' sluggish approach than anything else. Whatever the prognosis of the pundits, Forest still ended up with both points to put towards their assault on the First Division title.

The win over the Foxes was just what the doctor ordered, putting Forest six points clear at the top of the table. The players were now again in a confident frame of mind, as four days later Forest took on Liverpool in their first cup final since 1959. The Reds versus the Reds.

Archie Gemmill was born in Paisley on 24 March 1947. He joined St Mirren, before moving to Preston North End and Derby County, where he became one of Clough and Taylor's key players in the title-winning Rams side of the mid-1970s. Eventually Clough got his man for Forest in September 1977, making his debut for the Reds against Norwich City on 1 October 1977. Archie went on to make 58 League appearances for Forest, including 2 as substitute, scoring 4 goals.

The dynamic skills of midfielder Archie Gemmill graced many stadiums all over the world. He won 43 Scottish caps, scoring 8 goals. His greatest accolade was to be the scorer of a fantastic goal for Scotland against eventual runners-up Holland in the 3-2 group stage victory in the 1978 World Cup finals in Argentina. Rob Resenbrink had put the Dutchmen 1-0 up from the penalty spot (incidentally, this was the 1,000th World Cup goal). Rioch headed against the bar and Dalglish had a goal disallowed, before netting the equaliser, then Souness was pushed over in the box and Archie scored from the resultant spot kick. The ubiquitous Archie then weaved past three defenders to score one of the goals of the tournament to make it 3-1. Sadly, for the Scots, who needed to win by at least three clear goals, Johnny Rep struck a twenty-five-yard thunderbolt to bring the final score to 3-2.

Clough left Archie out of the 1979 European Cup-winning team, obviously upsetting the wee man to the extent that Gemmill was sold to Birmingham City in August 1979. Many believe that Archie Gemmill was discarded far too soon by Cloughie. After Birmingham, he spent a little time with Jacksonville before signing for Wigan Athletic, and subsequently for a second spell at Derby County, where he teamed up with manager Peter Taylor.

Nottingham Forest: Shilton, Anderson, Clark, O'Hare, Needham, Burns, O'Neill, Gemmill, Bowyer, Woodcock, Robertson. Sub: Lloyd

Leicester City: Wallington, Whitworth, Rofe, Kelly, Sims (Davies), Webb, Weller, Hughes, Christie, Salmons, Williams.

Nottingham Forest v. Liverpool

Football League Cup final, Wembley
Attendance: 100,000

Date: Saturday 18 March 1978
Referee: Mr P. Partridge (County Durham)

Brian Clough proudly led out his Nottingham Forest team to face the mighty Liverpool, to contest the first domestic trophy of the season. His previous experience of this was as the manager of 'Don Revie's' Leeds United for the 1974 FA Charity Shield, (the game infamous for the sending off of Bremner and Keegan). This time Cloughie was here on merit. Forest's opponents were Bob Paisley's multiple trophy-winning Liverpool side. The legendary Scousers were pretty good, to say the least. Forest were very much the underdogs.

On the injury front, Skipper John McGovern and Colin Barrett were given late fitness tests. McGovern made it, however, Barrett didn't. So with Peter Shilton, Archie Gemmill and Dave Needham all cup-tied, the 'Dynamic Duo' hadn't too many players to choose from. Peter Withe returned to the team after missing the game against Leicester. As in all League Cup ties since the second round, Chris Woods took Shilton's place in Forest's goal. At 18 years and 124 days, Woods was reputed to be the youngest-ever goalkeeper to appear in a major Wembley final. Frank Clark played at left-back, with Ian Bowyer coming into midfield.

As was expected, Liverpool attacked from the off, and Chris Woods had to demonstrate his athleticism and agility, as he pulled off a string of fantastic saves to keep out efforts from Kenny Dalglish and Terry McDermott. The best of the bunch was his brilliant one-handed save from a fierce Emlyn Hughes' shot that Woods turned around the post. The young 'keeper followed up with a marvellous block to keep out a Kenny Dalglish effort from point-blank range, before going on to make numerous saves and blocks. Dalglish had already scored six goals in this competition. Forest came close to scoring when McGovern laid a beautiful ball into the run of Martin O'Neill. The Irishman forced his way into the corner of the penalty box, took aim and rifled a ferocious shot just wide of Clemence's right-hand post. Then Robertson split the Liverpool defence with a delightful pass to Tony Woodcock, but before the youngster could set himself for a shot, he was hacked down by Tommy Smith. Unfortunately, the free-kick came to nothing.

Things were starting to look quite good for Forest, until Steve Heighway ran clear, before floating the ball into the box, where Viv Anderson was thankful to put it behind for a corner. The resultant cross was cleared without difficulty. The game was developing into a splendid advertisement for English football, and thus far, Forest had effectively dealt with Liverpool's attacks, and had created a number of good chances of their own. In their next raid, Woodcock ran intelligently to open up the Liverpool defence, before squaring the ball across the edge of the box. Withe raced in to meet the ball, but Smith got there first, to boot the ball away. Then, from an inch-perfect cross, Peter Withe headed straight at Clemence. If he had misheaded, it would have been a certain goal.

Opposite: The front cover of the match-day programme.

Score after extra time:

Nottingham Forest 0   **Liverpool 0**

FOOTBALL LEAGUE CUP FINAL
Saturday 18 March 1978 · 3pm

LIVERPOOL V NOTTINGHAM FOREST

Wembley Stadium

FABULOUS FOREST!

CLOUGH'S MEN ON THE GLORY TRAIL

IT SURPRISES NO ONE, LEAST OF ALL THEIR MANAGER, THAT NOTTINGHAM FOREST WILL WALK ON TO THE TURF AT WEMBLEY STADIUM THIS AFTER- NOON FOR THEIR FIRST APPEARANCE IN A FOOTBALL LEAGUE CUP FINAL. AND IF AT APPROXIMATELY 4.45 P.M. THEIR PLAYERS ARE DOING A CANTER OF TRIUMPH AROUND THE PERIMETER OF THE PITCH, THAT WILL SURPRISE FEW EITHER, EVEN THOUGH THEY WILL HAVE BEATEN MIGHTY LIVERPOOL.

For nothing seems to be beyond the capabilities of Nottingham Forest this season.

In just seven months they have taken the First Division by storm and have also served notice of their ability to win sterling silver for the trophy cabinet at the City Ground this season and in future years.

Their success this season represents one of the most astonishing transformations of a team in modern football history.

★ ★ ★

THEY did only just enough to win promotion at the end of last season, clinching third place in Division II behind Wolverhampton Wanderers and Chelsea, ahead of a clutch of rivals, notably Bolton Wanderers and Black- pool.

Their elevation was accomplished with a brand of football master-minded by their manager BRIAN CLOUGH and orchestrated by his assistant PETER TAYLOR, a partnership as dynamic to soccer as Tate is to Lyle in the sugar industry and Rolls is to Royce in the motor trade.

Few doubted that Forest's brand of stylish, attack- ing football would succeed in the higher echelons of the Football League's top division, but would the players simply hold their own or win some titles this season?

Manager: Brian Clough

Manager Clough was adamant. Forest were good, very good, but not good enough.

So, while less forthright managers would have given a promotion-winning side the benefit of an extended trial in the hope they might make the grade, **CLOUGH** took no chances, moving swiftly and boldly into the transfer market to build a team that has done remarkably well in all competitions this season.

★ ★ ★

PETER TAYLOR Assistant Manager

ROUND-BY-ROUND TO WEMBLEY

First Round		Bye
Second Round	West Ham United (H) (O'Neill, Bowyer 2, Woodcock, Withe)	5–0
Third Round	Notts County (H) (Robertson pen., Woodcock, Bowyer 2)	4–0
Fourth Round	Aston Villa (H) (Lloyd, Anderson, Withe, Woodcock)	4–2
Fifth Round	Bury (A) (Bowyer, O'Neill, Robertson)	3–0
Semi-Final	Leeds United (A) (Withe 2, O'Hare)	3–1
Semi-Final	Leeds United (H) (Withe, Bowyer, O'Neill, Woodcock)	4–2
Goalscorers:	Bowyer 6, Withe 5, Woodcock 4, O'Neill 3, Robertson 2, Lloyd 1, Anderson 1, O'Hare 1. Total 23.	

An extract from the match-day programme.

Forest redoubled their efforts, and only a timely thirty-yard dash from his goal line by Clemence saved the Scousers. His well-timed sprint got him to the ball just as it reached Woodcock. The Reds really should have taken the lead in the thirty-seventh minute, when Ian Bowyer was put clear. Forest's flame-haired midfielder rifled in a rising shot from twenty yards, which had Clemence beaten, but skimmed the crossbar. Two minutes after this let off, Liverpool had the ball in the Forest net. Terry McDermott received the ball on the edge of the Forest area and hit a low shot that skidded across the slick Wembley surface. His shot beat the diving Woods and curled into the corner of the net. Liverpool's players and fans went crazy with joy. Well, for a few seconds at least. They hadn't heard referee Pat Partridge's whistle, but now turned to see the official indicating that the Liverpool goalscorer had been offside when receiving the ball; it was tough on Liverpool. McDermott couldn't believe it, he had scored what he thought was a good goal. After this, the remainder of the half was pretty much all Liverpool. With half-time approaching, Forest put in one final attack. John Robertson's surging run took him to the edge of the Liverpool penalty area, but was crowded out as he shaped to shoot.

In the second half, most pundits reported that Forest were simply outplayed by the Merseysiders, who emerged after the break to set up a barrage of non-stop attacks. An early cross saw Woods leap magnificently to cut out the danger, and although his clearance set up a quick Forest attack, Liverpool were soon snapping back on the offensive.

Woods was soon called upon to make another save. Ray Kennedy fired in a fearsome drive that the Forest 'keeper made look simple by readjusting his feet with lightning speed to get his body behind the ball. They say that fortune favours the brave, and certainly, Woods deserved the slice of luck that came his way minutes later. Diving at full stretch to keep out another thunderbolt from Kennedy, the ball bounced off the 'keeper's chest and spun towards Dalglish, who looked odds on to score. However, Woods managed to scramble across to push the ball away, hurting his hand in the process.

The pressure from Liverpool was relentless. Next, Steve Heighway set up Dalglish with a slide-rule pass into the Forest penalty area. The Scottish ace turned on the ball in an instant to smash in a shot that Woods did well to keep out. The pace of Liverpool's attacks was breathtaking, players surging forward at every opportunity, but each time Forest's defenders were equal to the task. Emlyn Hughes was now getting into some great forward positions, forcing first Burns and then Clark to block shots. Then 'Crazy Horse' slipped a fabulous ball into McDermott's run. The England midfielder thundered in a haymaker of a shot that had Woods scrambling to keep the ball out his net.

It was all Liverpool. They were beating Forest in most areas of the vast Wembley pitch, especially in midfield where McGovern in particular looked to be struggling. Forest just couldn't get going, and even when they did finally manage to break away, there was no understanding between the players, who were constantly getting in each other's way. Nevertheless, Liverpool still hadn't scored, and the clock was ticking away. Then referee Partridge blew the whistle for time.

Liverpool brought on super-sub David Fairclough at the start of extra-time in place of Ray Kennedy, and began as they had left off after ninety minutes. In the first attack, Kenny Burns got across smartly to block a shot from Phil Neal. Then at the end of another mazy run, Steve Heighway fired narrowly wide. Following a few minutes of unproductive midfield play, Fairclough and

Nottingham Forest v. Liverpool

Dalglish combined to set up McDermott. But once again, the superb Woods was on hand, diving onto McDermott's shot. Forest weren't out of it that was certain, and came back with a run and cross from Martin O'Neill. The ball dropped near the box, which Larry Lloyd won tigerishly to make an opening for Woodcock who unfortunately placed his effort wide of the post.

The remainder of extra time came and went without too much danger, and Forest lived to fight another day. Their defence had been resolute, maybe a little lucky at times. However, despite having enough chances to have won by a street, Liverpool's stars had been kept at bay. But remember, it's them that guz in, uz counts, me ducks! Overnight, young Chris Woods became the hero of heroes. Four days later they would have to do it all again.

Some pundits called this a bit of a drab game; they must have been nuts as well as blind!

In the midst of these cup games, let's remind ourselves what the top of the League table looked like. Whilst the cat was away a few of the mice collected a couple of points; Arsenal beat Bristol City 4-1, Coventry drew 1-1 at Ipswich, Leeds won 5-0 against Middlesbrough, Manchester City drew 1-1 at Wolves, and Albion drew 1-1 at Old Trafford, Everton didn't play:

	PLD	W	D	L	F	A	PTS
Forest	**30**	**20**	**7**	**3**	**55**	**18**	**47**
Everton	32	16	10	6	58	36	42
Man City	32	17	7	8	59	36	41
Arsenal	32	16	8	8	45	27	40
Liverpool	31	16	6	9	42	28	38
Leeds	32	15	8	9	50	37	38

By way of a diversion, the Cloughie and Taylor once again applied their own unique brand of preparation for a major game. This time, they took the squad to Scarborough for few days of relaxation.

Nottingham Forest: Woods, Anderson, Clark, McGovern (O'Hare), Lloyd, Burns, O'Neill, Bowyer, Withe, Woodcock, Robertson.
Liverpool: Clemence, Neal, Smith, Thompson P., Kennedy (Fairclough), Hughes, Dalglish, Case, Heighway, McDermott, Callaghan.

NOTTINGHAM FOREST v. LIVERPOOL

Football League Cup final replay, Old Trafford   **Date:** 22 March 1978
Attendance: 54,375   **Referee:** Mr P. Partridge (County Durham)

It's strange that in the two games of the final, plus extra time in the first game, two free-scoring teams like Forest and Liverpool only managed one goal between them. Forest had scored 23 goals on their way to the final, to Liverpool's 13.

Ray Kennedy had recovered from a stomach upset, enabling Liverpool to field an unchanged team. Not so Forest. McGovern, who been substituted in the second half of Saturday's game, had to stay in Nottingham for treatment on his groin strain while his colleagues enjoyed a bracing couple of days in Scarborough. Most pundits felt that Forest would be more at home at Old Trafford than the wide open spaces of Wembley, with its energy-sapping turf. With John O'Hare coming in for McGovern, Cloughie named young Steve Elliott as substitute. Forest lined up with four in midfield, John Robertson playing in a slightly withdrawn role to combat Liverpool's creative threat from the middle of the park. Larry Lloyd and Kenny Burns were immense, and behind them in goal was the hero of the first game, young Chris Woods.

Once again, Chris Woods came to Forest's rescue early on, with two magnificent saves in the first twelve minutes from Neal and Dalglish. The first came on ten minutes, when Woods dived full-length to keep out a fierce drive from Phil Neal, and then two minutes later, leaped sideways at full stretch to clasp a shot from Kenny Dalglish. Then Woodcock laid on a glorious early chance for Withe, but the big striker headed over from six yards, followed by a speculative twenty-yarder from Ian Bowyer that flew into the arms of Clemence. On the half-hour mark, Liverpool's best chance so far was wasted by Kenny Dalglish. The Scottish ace sped into the area but shot tamely at goal.

Much of the game was being played in a crowded midfield, in a contest that at times resembled a game of chess. Withe was booked in the thirty-fourth minute for a foul on Phil Thompson, and five minutes later Anderson suffered the same fate after scything down Steve Heighway. The silliest of the three cautions was when thirty-five-year-old Ian Callaghan was booked for the most innocuous of body-checks on Peter Withe; Callaghan's first ever caution in 849 first-team appearances. Nil-nil at half-time probably flattered Forest, but it's about goals, and Liverpool still hadn't scored any.

The second period began, with both teams probing for an opening. It was a fifty-second-minute John Robertson penalty that finally broke the deadlock. John O'Hare was put through by Tony Woodcock, who slipped a lovely ball into his path. The big striker latched on to the ball, and was in full flight on his way into Liverpool's penalty area, when Phil Thompson's cynical, so-called 'professional' foul, stopped him in his tracks. Referee Pat Partridge pointed to the spot without hesitation; penalty to Forest – or goal, as was usually the outcome, for Robertson rarely missed. Forest's left-winger placed his spot kick well wide of Ray Clemence.

With the benefit of modern electronic gadgetry, one might say that technically the foul was committed just outside the area; however, a penalty was definitely merited in this case. Robbo had

---

Nottingham Forest 1   **Liverpool 0**
  Robertson (penalty 52)

NOTTINGHAM FOREST V. LIVERPOOL

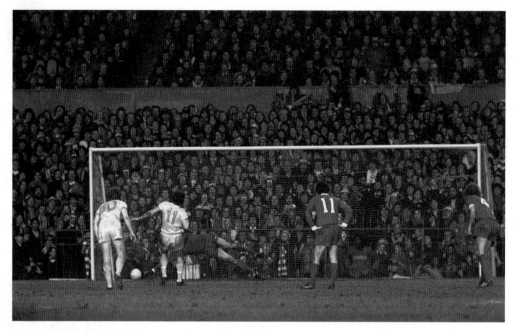

John Robertson slides the winning penalty past the diving Ray Clemence.

caressed the ball into the net to make it 1-0 to Forest. In the fifty-seventh minute, Terry McDermott got the ball in the net again, and again it was disallowed, this time for hands. You might say that Liverpool were not best pleased. They dominated this game as they had the first encounter, but had only themselves to blame after three-and-a-half hours of play in which a multitude of chances were missed.

Nottingham Forest had won their first trophy for years, thanks to Clough and Taylor, not forgetting the players, of course. It was a marvellous effort. A great victory. A just reward for the scintillating football that Forest had played all season. And, remember, this was a game where Forest were denied the services of five first-team players.

Fantastic, stupendous, wonderful, marvellous and loads more besides. Nottingham Forest had won the Football League Cup, and in doing so had qualified for Europe. Next season it would be the UEFA Cup! However Forest were still top of the League; maybe, just maybe, it might be the European Cup.

Returning to League action, Forest's next victims, sorry, opponents, were the Geordies, who were in desperate trouble at the foot of the table

---

Nottingham Forest: Woods, Anderson, Clark, O'Hare, Lloyd, Burns, O'Neill, Bowyer, Withe, Woodcock, Robertson. Sub: Elliott

Liverpool: Clemence, Neal, Smith, Thompson P., Kennedy, Hughes, Dalglish, Case (Fairclough), Heighway, McDermott, Callaghan.

Forest's John Robertson, Kenny Burns, Viv Anderson and Tony Woodcock parade the League Cup around Old Trafford.

Eighteen year-old reserve **Chris Woods** got his chance in Forest's Football League Cup side because Peter Shilton was cup-tied. In the Final at Wembley, the young man gave a commanding display to keep a clean sheet. In the replay, he was just as composed, as Forest beat Liverpool to lift this trophy for the first time.

Chris was born in Boston, Lincs, on 14 November 1959, making his Forest debut against Notts County on 25 October 1977, at the tender age of 17 years, 11 months. Clough surprised the football world in July 1979, by transferring his young League Cup winner to QPR before he had even played a League game at Forest. Woods then joined Norwich City, first on –loan, then officially in July 1981, for a fee of £250,000, before moving to Glasgow Rangers in July 1986, for a fee of £600,000. At Norwich, Chris won the League Cup for the second time, plus a Division 2 Championship medal. With Rangers, he won four Scottish Premiership titles and three Scottish League Cups.

In August 1991, he was transferred to newly promoted First Division Sheffield Wednesday for a then record fee of £1.2 million, helping the Owls to third place in the League in his first season. Wednesday were also the losing finalists in both domestic cup competitions, the following year.

Woods was loaned out to Reading in 1995, before moving on a free transfer to Colorado Rapids, and subsequently Southampton, Sunderland and Burnley, from where he retired in August 1998. On the international scene, Chris Woods went on to win 43 full England caps, to add to his haul of 'B', Under-21 and Youth caps.

Nottingham Forest v. Newcastle United

Football League First Division, City Ground
Attendance: 35,552

Date: Easter Saturday, 25 March 1978
Referee: Mr N.H. Glover (Chorley)

Another double, this time over the Geordie boys. John Robertson scored his fifth penalty in eight games. A surprisingly low turnout welcomed the League Cup winners back home.

Skipper John McGovern's groin injury still hadn't improved, so once again John O'Hare deputised. Ten minutes before the kick-off, the crowd gave McGovern a fantastic reception when he ran out with the Football League Cup held proudly on high for all Forest fans to see.

Newcastle were first to attack but Frank Clark cleared the danger. Then Robertson tricked Barton, but Blackley stretched to boot away his cross. Playing against his former club, Frank Clark, who had never scored a League goal in his entire career, nearly changed the record books in Forest's next attack. Running on to a Robbo through ball he swapped passes with Withe, before thundering a goal-bound shot that was kicked off the line. Woodcock followed up, but his effort was also blocked. Young Newcastle defender David Barton took a nasty knock, which needed lengthy treatment. Newcastle were looking lively, and Alan Kennedy combined well with Mark McGhee, before whipping in a fine effort that hit a Forest defender and bounced to safety.

Robbo was providing plenty of thrust down the left, and in the next raid found Woodcock, who fired in a hard low cross from near the byline that Mike Mahoney managed to catch at the far post. Then following a silly mistake by Ken Mitchell, Gemmill pounced on the ball. The Scot sped at the Geordies' defence then slid in a nice-looking ball that was unfortunately inches ahead of Withe. Next, after Peter Withe had won the ball from John Bird, O'Neill tried to get through, but John Blackley took the ball from him before he could get into the area. Minutes later, Robbo forced Irving Nattrass to concede a left-wing corner. Woodcock was first to the ball to smack a low shot, which ricocheted clear.

Forest pressed again, and Robbo shimmied onto his right foot to explode a drive that slammed against Nulty's head; it must have hurt. Then, O'Hare smashed his shot against Woodcock. Now it was Newcastle's turn to have a go. McGhee won a corner off Frank Clark, but from Barrowclough's centre Bird headed wide. Straight after, Robbo easily turned Nattrass before whipping over a cross-cum-shot that had Mahoney diving across his goal to save. Then, the Newcastle 'keeper plucked a powerful header from Dave Needham from under the crossbar.

Although Forest were well in control, they were certainly struggling to make the ultimate breakthrough. The Red's frustration seemed to manifest itself in a growing confidence for the Newcastle players, who before the game would surely have been thrilled to get a draw against the League leaders. Sensing a possible upset the Geordies swept downfield. Only a fantastic save by Peter Shilton prevented a goal. Ken Mitchell won the ball on the edge of the Forest area, before sliding it for McGhee to crash in a rising shot that the Forest 'keeper palmed brilliantly over the crossbar.

Nottingham Forest 2
  Robertson (penalty 32),
  Anderson (67)

Newcastle United 0

Nottingham Forest v. Newcastle United

Viv Anderson.

Forest knew they had to do something, and swarmed back on the attack. In the thirty-second minute, John O'Hare made ground before slipping the ball through into the area. Woodcock latched onto the ball and went over under a challenge from Nattrass and Kennedy. 'Penalty' said the referee. Hmmm. His controversial decision certainly seemed harsh to the Newcastle lads. The most vociferous protest came from Nattrass, who spoke too strongly and was booked. This was Forest's third penalty in as many games; who said that refs weren't angels in disguise? Up stepped the penalty king to send Mahoney the wrong way with his usual aplomb. It was Robbo's ninth League goal of the season.

The goal gave Forest an extra spring in their step. The meanest defence in the League wasn't about to surrender this hard-won lead. Anderson stopped McGhee with a great tackle, then Shilton just about managed to fist Barrowclough's corner over after he had advanced a bit too far out of his goal. Nattrass robbed Woodcock inside the area, following a neat move between O'Neill and Gemmill, and then just before the interval Barton crashed into Woodcock to earn himself a booking. Half-time: 1-0 to Forest.

Forest came out for the second half determined to extend their lead. Robbo fed Woodcock six yards out and the young striker spun on a tanner to slide the ball into the path of the onrushing O'Hare, whose first-time drive was turned behind by the diving Mahoney. Then for the second time in as many minutes, Mahoney had to be sharp to keep out a great header from Needham. Newcastle's massed defence now took on a siege-like mentality. Needham whipped in a free-kick, and Withe twisted to power in a header that the leaping Mahoney grabbed gratefully.

Newcastle attacks were almost as rare as rocking-horse droppings. However, from one, Barraclough sent over a dangerous cross from the left that Mitchell glanced well wide. Then McGhee forced a corner off Burns, only to see Blackley miss his header, and Robertson clear comfortably. That was pretty much it as far as Newcastle attacks went, and now Robertson got Forest moving, but his cross was scrambled clear by Barton. Then Gemmill found Withe who snapped in a shot that Mahoney smothered at the foot of the post. Newcastle had a third player booked when Kennedy hotly disputed the referee's decision after a foul by Bird. Forest were back again, and this time O'Neill crossed from the right, but although Robertson got in a shot, the ball went harmlessly wide. Eventually Forest's unrelenting pressure paid off. In the sixty-seventh minute, Archie Gemmill cracked in a super effort that crashed against the bar before rebounding dangerously downwards, forcing Mahoney to dive to his right to push the ball away. The Newcastle goalie was out of luck because the ball came to Viv Anderson, who forced it home.

Seconds later, Newcastle almost pulled a goal back, when Kennedy tried to lob Shilton. Fortunately, Shilts managed to get back to acrobatically tip the ball over. Towards the end of the game, O'Neill burst through to set up Withe, but again Forest's number nine was thwarted as this time his shot was blocked by Bird. Goal number three looked to have arrived when Burns leaped to meet Robbo's corner, but his glancing header skimmed the post. Withe looped a shot over the bar, before O'Neill screwed a late right-foot effort wide of target.

The League table:

	PLD	W	D	L	F	A	PTS
Forest	**31**	**21**	**7**	**3**	**57**	**18**	**49**
Everton	34	18	10	6	62	36	46
Arsenal	34	17	9	8	48	28	43
Man City	33	17	8	8	61	38	42
Liverpool	32	17	6	9	45	29	40
Coventry	33	16	8	9	63	51	40

Forest were back in the North-East four days later for a trip to Cloughie's home town, and the club where he had originally made his name with his fantastic goalscoring feats for Middlesbrough and Sunderland.

Nottingham Forest: Shilton, Anderson (Bowyer), Clark, O'Hare, Needham, Burns K., O'Neill, Gemmill, Withe, Woodcock, Robertson.

Newcastle United: Mahoney, Nattrass, Kennedy A., Barton, Bird, Blackley, Barrowclough, Nulty, Mitchell, McGhee, Walker. Sub: Burns M.

MIDDLESBROUGH v. NOTTINGHAM FOREST

Football League First Division, Ayresome Park   **Date:** Wednesday 29 March 1978
Attendance: 25,445   **Referee:** Mr N. Midgley (Salford)

Viv Anderson hadn't recovered from injury, so Ian Bowyer came in at right-back, with John O'Hare still deputising for John McGovern. Boro were hoping to bounce back from their 1-0 home defeat by Leicester on Easter Monday, and certainly scared the League leaders with an all-action display in this pulsating draw. There's little doubt that Forest were the happier of the two sides at the final whistle, having got out of jail a couple of times, and then to have miraculously survived in the final minutes when David Mills missed a sitter.

The first scoring chance fell to Forest inside the first ten minutes. From a fairly innocuous ball, David Mills stupidly miskicked straight to John O'Hare, who cleverly swept the ball into the run of Martin O'Neill. The Irishman made ground and drilled in a low shot that glanced past the post off a defender. The corner led to nothing, and three minutes later, Forest were a goal down. Dave Armstrong collected a throw-in, cut inside past Bowyer, eased his way into the corner of the penalty area, and slipped a perfect pass for David Mills to rifle the ball into the net off Shilton's body.

Forest showed their fighting spirit with an immediate response. Tony Woodcock raced through the Boro defence in characteristic fashion, before holding off the nearest defender to crack in a fierce drive that flashed narrowly wide of the post. A couple of minute's later Forest were back in it. Kenny Burns swapped passes with Frank Clark and released the ball to Archie Gemmill who touched it on to Woodcock. The young Forest striker took the ball wide of out-rushing Boro 'keeper David Brown and calmly slotted it home for the equaliser. Having got back to level terms, Forest should have probably shut up shop for a while in order to draw breath. They didn't of course, and went behind again two minutes later.

Armstrong's curling free-kick was met by Billy Ashcroft, who beat Dave Needham in the air to direct a neat header to Stan Cummins, for the little Geordie to fire past Shilton from close in. Alan Ramage was at the centre of a couple of heart-stopping moments for Boro. First, he got across to block a fierce shot from John Robertson. Then, ten minutes before the break, almost lobbed the ball into his own net. Forest were still striving for the equaliser and went very close following a Robertson corner, when Ian Bailey booted Martin O'Neill's goal-bound effort off the line. Half-time: 2-1 to Middlesbrough.

Ian Bailey set up Boro's first chance after the interval, sending in a bouncing centre that Mills did well to control and send just past the woodwork all in one movement. Forest hit back with a driving move in which Withe combined beautifully with Bowyer to set up Martin O'Neill. The Irish midfielder collected the ball to fire past the unsighted Brown to bring the score to 2-2. Now Forest sensed a win, and threw everything at the home side. Fifteen minutes from time, Bowyer fired Woodcock's short corner across the box for Needham to glance down to Robbo. The Scot zipped in a humdinger of a shot that must have shaken the nuts off the bolts holding the crossbar to the posts.

Middlesbrough 2	Nottingham Forest 2
Mills (13), Cummins (22)	Woodcock (20), O'Neill (54)

MIDDLESBROUGH V. NOTTINGHAM FOREST

Martin O'Neill.

But now, back to Mills' phenomenal miss. Billy Ashcroft went clear and sent in what looked to be the perfect centre for the incoming David Mills. He must score. It was impossible to miss. But miss he did. With an empty net gaping wider than a whale's mouth, he nodded the ball the wrong side of the post from Boro's point of view, and suddenly it was all over. Forest had hung on to grab a vital point. To be fair, they always looked as though they had goals in them in what had been one of their toughest games for some time. Kenny Burns picked up his first booking of the season for bringing down Stan Cummins and then time-wasting to prevent a quick free-kick. Mills was booked for dissent.

Next up was a chance to avenge the November defeat at the hands of the pensioners from Stamford Bridge.

Middlesbrough: Brown, Craggs, Bailey, Mahoney, Boam, Ramage, Mills, Cummins, Ashcroft, McAndrew, Armstrong. Sub: Hickton
Nottingham Forest: Shilton, Bowyer, Clark, O'Hare, Needham, Burns, O'Neill, Gemmill, Withe, Woodcock, Robertson. Sub: Barrett

Nottingham Forest v. Chelsea

Football League First Division, City Ground
Attendance: 31,262

Date: Saturday 1 April 1978
Referee: Mr G. Nolan (Stockport)

Chelsea were the April fools after Forest came back from a goal down to win the game with two late goals. In the continued absence of Anderson, Ian Bowyer again played at right-back, with John O'Hare continuing to deputise for John McGovern. Larry Lloyd regained his place in the starting line-up at the expense of Dave Needham, whose recent form had dropped below what was expected. Forest opened brightly, and in the first attack of the game Robertson whipped in a left-wing cross that sailed past attackers and defenders alike to glide narrowly beyond the far post. Moments later, in the third minute, Bowyer switched the ball onto his left foot to float in a centre that Robertson headed past the post.

The Londoners looked a little toothless, and when Walker and Lewington combined to create an opening for Langley, Bowyer comfortably turned the ball back to Shilton. Then against the run of play, Chelsea bared their teeth and stunned the visitors with a goal after eight minutes. Harris swerved a free-kick into the Forest area, which was met perfectly by Micky Droy. Shilton uncharacteristically fumbled the ball, and Langley was first on the scene to poke out a leg to push the ball across the line. Forest's determination to regain the initiative produced a number of half-chances. Larry Lloyd whacked in long-range effort that hit Woodcock, but unfortunately ricocheted just ahead of Martin O'Neill. Down the left, Robbo was creating his normal brand of chaos, but a series of crosses and corners saw the dominant Micky Droy stand firm to clear every ball that came anywhere near him.

In a rare Chelsea counterattack, Britton fed Finnieston, and although his shot bounced nastily, Shilton managed to grab the ball at the second attempt. Forest swept back upfield, and only a goal-line clearance prevented an equaliser. Kenny Burns met Robbo's corner to power in a header that Clive Walker booted off the line. Minutes later, Woodcock forced Wicks to concede another corner, but this time the referee judged that Lloyd and Burns had sandwiched Bonetti as he came out to collect. The pensioners were unable to break out of their own half as Forest increased their stranglehold on the game. Woodcock shimmied past Wicks but slammed his left-footer wide. Next, Frank Clark tried his luck after swapping passes with Woodcock. Sadly, the Geordie smashed his shot into Bonetti's knees. From another Robertson corner, Lloyd looped a header over the bar, then almost immediately afterwards stretched to reach a Burns free-kick, which again Chelsea managed to scramble away.

Eventually Chelsea got the ball forward, but Britton, running in on goal, put his shot wide. Lewington and Britton combined well to create another chance that Bowyer put behind for a corner. When the ball came in, Withe beat Droy to the ball to head clear. Then Kenny Swain attempted to catch Shilton out with a long-range effort, but England's real number one saved easily. Chelsea's resurgence quickly burned out in the face of some determined play by Forest, who now

Nottingham Forest 3
  Burns (68), O'Neill (82),
  Robertson (87)

Chelsea 1
  Langley (8)

Martin O'Neill.

sped back to the attack. A minute before half-time, Lloyd and Burns went up for another Robbo corner, resulting in Tony Woodcock flashing the ball into the Chelsea net. However, Forest's joy was short-lived as the referee judged that Bonetti had been obstructed as he jumped for the ball. Then Woodcock ran through the home defence, but was robbed of the ball by the excellent Droy. Half-time: 1-0 to Chelsea.

At the start of the second half Kenny Swain showed his composure, first hooking the ball clear from Burns, and then heading O'Neill's cross behind. Robbo's corner-kick was easily cleared. However, the pressure on the Blues' goal was mounting. 'Chopper' Harris upended Withe just outside the area, only for Burns to completely miss his kick when the ball was squared to him. Forest's next corner produced another anxious moment for the visitors. The ball rebounded to Robbo, who took it to the byline before whipping in a teasing cross that Larry Lloyd met perfectly to power in a header that Clive Walker again blocked on the line. From the clearance, Chelsea might have increased their lead. Ian Britton's right-wing cross sailed over Bowyer's head to the feet of Walker, who pulled his first-time shot across goal and the ball flew wide of the far post.

Despite this near miss, the Reds were well on top; surely, they must score soon. Twice in quick succession, they almost made the breakthrough. First Woodcock sent in a well-placed header that had Bonetti diving across his goal to make the catch. Then O'Neill cleverly beat Harris on the corner of the area, before blasting a right-foot shot that was inches outside the far post. Chelsea broke out again, and the impressive Swain sent Walker clear. This time Shilton dived to his right to smother the ball. The action swung back to the Chelsea end, and Bonetti needed to be alert to prevent a goal by Forest. Withe found Woodcock, who came back onto to his right-foot to rifle in a shot that had the Chelsea 'keeper flying to his left to make the save.

Forest's management decided that a change of formation might have the desired effect, and sent on Barrett to replace Gemmill. Barrett slotted in at right-back with Bowyer moving into midfield. And thankfully the ploy worked. The change added even greater impetus to Forest's attacking ideas, and nearly brought a goal. When Robbo's cross deflected off John O'Hare, there was Martin O'Neill to volley narrowly wide. A couple of minutes later, Forest's unrelenting pressure earned its reward. In the sixty-eighth minute, Robertson swung over a corner from the left, Burns rose to meet the ball and powered in a header that hit the post and a defender on its way into the net.

Now Forest laid siege to the Londoners goal and, scenting blood, O'Neill was first to put it to the test with a stinging right-foot shot that looked in all the way until the ball brushed a defender to pass behind for a corner. Forest maintained their barrage, and scored a brilliant second goal. On eighty-two minutes, Frank Clark laid the ball into the path of Martin O'Neill, and the Irishman let fly with a thunderbolt that might have broken the net. Five minutes later, Robbo picked up the ball and ran straight at the Chelsea defence before thumping a great shot past Bonetti. With only three minutes remaining, there was no time for a shell-shocked Chelsea to recover, and Forest wrapped up the points.

The League table:

	PLD	W	D	L	F	A	PTS
Forest	**33**	**22**	**8**	**3**	**62**	**21**	**52**
Everton	36	20	10	6	66	38	50
Arsenal	36	18	10	8	53	29	46
Man City	35	18	9	8	65	41	45
Liverpool	33	18	6	9	48	29	42
Coventry	35	17	8	10	68	53	42

On Monday 3 April, Forest took on Derby County in another friendly, winning this encounter 2-1, with goals from Larry Lloyd and Ian Bowyer.

Nottingham Forest: Shilton, Bowyer, Clark, O'Hare, Lloyd, Burns, O'Neill, Gemmill (Barrett), Withe, Woodcock, Robertson.

Chelsea: Bonetti, Locke, Harris R., Britton, Droy, Wicks, Finnieston, Swain, Langley, Lewington, Walker. Sub: Frost

ASTON VILLA v. NOTTINGHAM FOREST

Football League First Division, Villa Park
Attendance: 44,315

Date: Wednesday 5 April 1978
Referee: Mr E. Hughes (Weston-super-Mare)

This was another reaffirmation of Greaves' classic phrase, 'It's a funny old game, Saint.' Newspapers called it 'An ambush, of which Robin Hood would have been proud, leaving Forest with the League title virtually signed, sealed and only to be delivered to the City Ground after Everton's one-nil defeat by Liverpool.'

Villa outplayed Forest all through this match, but could not score against Forest's resolute defence. Each attack was blunted either by some great tackling or by intuitive interceptions, and on many other occasions by the somewhat baffling decisions of referee Hughes. Fixing the blame firmly on the shoulders of the referee and his linesmen has become a bit of a national sport these days. However, in this case, an incensed Ron Saunders and his men appeared to have a legitimate cause for complaint. Unfortunately, most of his comments were unprintable!

For their part, Forest seemed content to sit back and let the home side do most of the work. According to the Villa manager, Mr Hughes' worst howler came after seventy-six minutes, when Kenny Burns appeared to punch Gordon Cowans' shot off the line. The Forest version goes like this – 'Gordon Cowans flighted what looked to be a perfect chip over Shilton's outstretched arms, only to watch in horror as Kenny Burns athletically hoofed the ball off the line.' The conditions in which this game was played were atrocious. Gale-force winds buffeted Villa Park to the extent that hard work and determination were more important than trying to play the ball around gracefully on the heavily sanded pitch. One wag said, 'The combination of Villa's notoriously bad pitch and the near tornado-strength wind, resembled the Sahara in a hurricane!'

Villa pressed the Forest defence from the kick-off, determined to extend their unbeaten run, with 'Dixie' Deehan and Denis Mortimer getting through copious amounts of work in a fighting midfield performance in which Frank Carrodus also shone. The swirling wind made it difficult to judge the flight of the ball, and resulted in a great many mistakes being made by both sides. Peter Shilton was once again at the top of his game, breaking the heart of Mortimer by pulling off a stunning save to keep out the midfielder's stinging volley. The score stayed at 0-0 until half-time.

The weather hadn't improved by the time the teams emerged for the second half. With the howling wind still making life difficult for the players the game descended rapidly into a bit of a non-event. A couple of Villa half-chances went begging, and as the game wore on, a draw seemed inevitable. Then four minutes from time came a move of breathtaking simplicity and speed that broke Villa hearts. In the eighty-sixth minute Robbo reached the byline before whipping in a wonderful cross that Woodcock headed cleanly past Rimmer. This fine goal won the game for Forest. Smash and grab? You'd better believe it!

Aston Villa 0

Nottingham Forest 1
Woodcock (86)

Tony Woodcock.

Four points ahead with eight games to play, and four games in hand over nearest rivals Everton. Dare Forest fans dream about the title?

On the following Saturday, 8 April, it was FA Cup semi-final day, and Forest hadn't got a game. Arsenal beat Orient 3-0 at Stamford Bridge, and Ipswich beat West Brom 3-1 at Highbury. In the League, Leeds were beaten 2-1 at home by West Ham, Coventry beat Everton 3-2, and Liverpool beat Leicester 3-2.

The League table:

	PLD	W	D	L	F	A	PTS
Forest	**34**	**23**	**8**	**3**	**63**	**21**	**54**
Everton	38	20	10	8	62	42	50
Arsenal	36	18	10	8	53	29	46
Liverpool	35	20	6	9	52	31	46
Man City	35	18	9	8	65	41	45
Coventry	37	18	9	10	71	55	45

Aston Villa: Rimmer, Gidman, Smith, Phillips, McNaught, Mortimer, Deehan, Little, Gray, Cowans, Carrodus. Sub: Gregory
Nottingham Forest: Shilton, Anderson, Barrett, O'Hare, Lloyd, Burns, O'Neill, Gemmill, Withe, Woodcock, Robertson. Sub: Bowyer

Manchester City v. Nottingham Forest

Football League First Division, Maine Road
Attendance: 43,428

Date: Tuesday 11 April 1978
Referee: Mr A. Hamil (Wolverhampton)

This game may have ended 0-0, but it was nonetheless yet another clean sheet for the impressive Reds, who simply purred their way through the entire ninety minutes.

Most pundits expected a goal-fest at one end or the other as both sides had already scored well in excess of sixty goals in the season so far. City had scored 41 goals at home and Forest had bagged 28 on their travels. The problem for City's all-star attack was that today they were face-to-face with the meanest defence in the League. Apart from the still injured John McGovern, Forest were at full strength, and in no mood to give away any goals. The Reds produced a thoroughly professional show of controlled football that saw Clough draw Robertson back into midfield in a 4-4-2 system that had been used to such great effect against Liverpool.

In the fifth minute, Robbo's fine pass sent Woodcock galloping into the box to chase the ball, but his shot squirmed away off Joe Corrigan in the City goal. Peter Withe was following up and reached the ball in time to crash in a fierce shot that rebounded to safety off Mike Doyle. At the other end, whenever the ever-reliable Peter Shilton was called into action, the England 'keeper was at his excellent best. Gary Owen dribbled his way into the area, before drilling his accurate shot wide of Shilts, or so it seemed until big Pete threw himself across goal to take the ball just inside the base of his right-hand post. Mike Doyle had already been up to his usual tricks, dishing out some ferocious challenges, mostly on Tony Woodcock. His latest of the series earned him an overdue and thoroughly deserved booking. Woodcock dusted himself off and in Forest's next attack nearly punished the City club captain, but screwed his shot wide of the upright. Then the England Under-21 striker had a great chance to put the Reds one up. John O'Hare slipped a slide-rule pass into the box for Woodcock to run on to, but as he shaped to shoot, Kenny Clements scythed him down. It looked a bolt-on penalty. However, the Forest players could only hold their heads in disbelief as referee Alex Hamil waved play on; he must have been unsighted, because if he had seen it he would surely have had no hesitation in awarding the spot kick. Half-time: 0-0.

After the interval, the game at times resembled a giant game of chess, with move and counter-move, even a couple of 'checks' came and went without either side managing the 'checkmate' that might have won it. City's defenders had definitely singled out Tony Woodcock as the main threat and continued to dish out some harsh treatment to the youngster. In one off-the-ball incident, Dave Watson appeared to hit Forest's number ten, but again, the referee's attention was elsewhere and Watson got away with his crime.

Woodcock wasn't about to be intimidated and hit back with another great run. Archie Gemmill put him through with a lovely pass, but as Tony was about to let fly, Paul Power managed to prod the ball away. City's best chance fell to Brian Kidd after Tommy Booth had won an aerial battle to nod the ball down into his path, but the former European Cup winner volleyed well over the bar.

Manchester City 0   Nottingham Forest 0

Soon after, following Robertson's corner, Martin O'Neill at the far post only just failed to connect with Peter Withe's header. There is no doubt that with a little bit more luck Forest would have come away from Maine Road with both points. All over the pitch they were the better side on display. At left-back, Colin Barrett made a mockery of the £30,000 fee that Cloughie had paid City for his services. Anderson and Burns played well, however the star of the show award must be given to Kenny Burns who once again turned in an almost faultless and commanding performance. His one error came when he drove a ferocious back-pass past his own post.

These famous five, with Shilton behind them, effectively shackled the precocious talents of Kidd, Channon and Barnes, keeping another clean sheet and maintaining an unbeaten record that now stretched to nineteen League games.

The League table:

	PLD	W	D	L	F	A	PTS
Forest	**35**	**23**	**9**	**3**	**63**	**21**	**55**
Everton	38	20	10	8	68	42	50
Arsenal	37	18	10	9	54	31	46
Liverpool	35	20	6	9	52	31	46
Man City	36	18	10	8	65	41	46

Leeds were seventh with 44 points from 38 games. West Brom had slipped to eighth.

The following evening, Wednesday 12 April, Forest were at Meadow Lane to beat neighbours Notts County 1-0. Substitute John O'Hare scored the only goal of a pretty dour affair.

Peter Withe stayed in the North-East until being bought by Aston Villa in May 1980 for a transfer fee of £500,000, where he won his second Championship winner's medal in 1980/81, scoring the winning goal for Villa in the European Champions Cup final in 1982, making 233 appearances for Villa and scoring a very creditable 92 goals. He was capped 11 times for England, scoring 1 goal, often teaming up with his former Forest strike partner Tony Woodcock. His first cap was against Brazil in 1981. His last was in the 8-0 thrashing of Turkey in the World Cup qualifying match in Istanbul, in an England team that included a few old Forest faces: Shilton, Anderson, Francis and Woodcock.

In July 1985, he moved on a free transfer to Sheffield United, and then went on-loan to Birmingham City between September and November 1987. He then went to Huddersfield Town as player-coach in July 1988, and subsequently in 1991 to Aston Villa as assistant manager/coach to Josef Venglos. From there Peter tried management with Wimbledon from October 1991 to January 1992. In a long career, Peter Withe played in excess of 600 games and scored more than 200 goals.

Manchester City: Corrigan, Clements, Power, Doyle, Watson, Owen, Channon, Booth, Kidd, Hartford, Barnes. Sub: Palmer

Nottingham Forest: Shilton, Anderson, Barrett, O'Hare, Lloyd, Burns, O'Neill, Gemmill, Withe, Woodcock, Robertson. Sub: Bowyer

Nottingham Forest v. Leeds United

Football League First Division, City Ground
Attendance: 38,662

Date: Saturday 15 April 1978
Referee: Mr A. McDonald (Birmingham)

Viv Anderson hadn't recovered from a knee injury and John O'Hare had been taken ill overnight, and with injured Tony Woodcock missing his first game of the season, Cloughie was forced to make changes. Barrett moved to right-back, Clark taking his place at left-back, McGovern returned, and Bowyer came in at number ten.

In the preceding November, Leeds, Cloughie's bête noire, were the last team to have beaten Forest in the League. Before the transfer deadline, Leeds had paid Blackpool £300,000 for central defender Paul Hart in an effort to shore up a defence that had capitulated under Forest's February League Cup onslaught.

Forest kicked-off, but were immediately under pressure from Leeds. Peter Hampton swung over a centre that Shilton managed to punch away from Eddie Gray. Then the Scot headed straight into Shilton's arms from a right-wing corner. Forest finally got onto the attack, winning a free-kick, which Robertson squared to Barrett, who thumped in a shot that Stewart caught cleanly. Shilton was soon back in action to prevent the visitors scoring. Eddie Gray took a Currie pass to the left before crossing into the box to Brian Flynn, who turned sharply to hammer a shot at goal. Fortunately, England's true number-one goalie sprang upwards to palm the ball over.

In Forest's next foray upfield, David Stewart had to be quick off his line to smother a cross-cum-shot from Robertson. The game now swung end-to-end, and Shilts was pleased to see a speculative thirty-yarder from Tony Currie fly past the angle. Then Hankin nodded Hampton's cross to Eddie Gray, but there was no power in his shot and Shilton fielded it comfortably. Seconds later, Flynn controlled a beautiful crossfield pass from Frankie Gray on the edge of the area, but thankfully, Gemmill managed to scramble across to whip the ball away.

After O'Neill had forced an unproductive corner, Currie's thoughtful pass sent Hampton away on the left, but the full-back's final ball was below par and Shilton easily gathered despite the close attentions of Ray Hankin. Then O'Neill and Withe combined to create an opening for McGovern, but the Forest skipper lost control of the ball before he could set himself. Leeds were straight back at Forest and Barrett had to resort to bringing down Arthur Graham to stop him. Although Hankin won Frankie Gray's free-kick in the air, his weak header was way off target. Leeds' goalkeeper David Stewart, who had been suffering from an injured foot all week and didn't take any goal kicks in this match, had to dive at full stretch to grab a ferocious shot from Robertson. Archie Gemmill was getting back to something approaching his best form, prompting Forest time and again, and it was he that set up the next Red's attack. Taking the ball round Madeley, the little Scot was halted in his tracks by a desperate clearance by Cherry. Next, Robbo floated in another inch-perfect cross for Withe to glance a header just past the post.

A nasty foul on Ian Bowyer looked like resulting in a booking for Paul Hart. He had already been spoken to by the referee following an earlier foul on Peter Withe. He was a lucky lad when the ref

---

Nottingham Forest 1
Withe (65)

Leeds United 1
Gray F. (penalty 41)

NOTTINGHAM FOREST

FOREST REVIEW
THE OFFICIAL MATCH-DAY
MAGAZINE OF NOTTINGHAM
FOREST FOOTBALL CLUB

Volume 10   Number 28

FOOTBALL LEAGUE DIVISION ONE

LEEDS UNITED
Saturday, 15th April, 1978
kick-off 3 p.m.

OFFICIAL
PROGRAMME   **15p**

The front cover of the match-day programme.

contented himself with a ticking-off. Leeds were still looking to score, and following Frank Gray's neat cross, Hankin tried a first-time volley that flashed past the woodwork. Now it was Forest's turn to go close. Paul Madeley made a hash of his clearance and Gemmill headed the ball on to Withe, who in turn found Bowyer, but when the cross came over to the far post, O'Neill sent his header the wrong side of the post.

The best save of the half came from Shilton. When Graham whipped over a dangerous-looking cross, the Forest 'keeper spectacularly tipped Hankin's excellent header over the crossbar. It didn't matter in the end because the referee blew for a foul against the Leeds striker. The brothers Gray had already posed a lot of problems for Forest, and now Frankie sent Eddie scurrying to the byline, before zipping in a low centre that Burns did well to intercept. There was no doubting that Forest were missing Woodcock up front, despite Bowyer doing an acceptable job in his absence. Then in the fortieth minute, after Lloyd had seen his shot pass well wide of the Leeds' goal, came a decision that stunned Forest's players and fans alike. After winning the ball in defence, skipper McGovern could only watch in horror as his clearance bounced off the referee to Brian Flynn. The Welshman chose to centre the ball rather than shoot. Eddie Gray and Colin Barrett both went for the ball and to everyone's surprise, referee McDonald blew for a forty-first minute penalty, ruling that Barrett had pushed the Scotsman. Forest's protests fell on deaf ears. Frankie Gray hammered his left-foot shot wide of Shilton to put Leeds ahead; a truly controversial penalty if there ever was one. In Forest's final attack of the half, Bowyer's header, from Robbo's left-wing centre, passed the wrong side of the post. Half-time: 1-0 to Leeds.

Leeds tried to slow the game down at the start of the second half, but after a frustrating few minutes Forest regained a little momentum. From another Robertson run and cross, off-balance Bowyer almost got in a shot from Withe's knock down. In came another cross from the left, but this time Hart was in the way to block McGovern's shot.

At the other end Leeds' appeals for a penalty for handball were refused by the referee, after Lloyd had blocked Arthur Graham's effort in the area. Then Tony Currie fed Eddie Gray on the right, only for the Scot's well-directed cross to be fired over by his brother Frank. Minutes later, in a momentary lapse of concentration, Lloyd allowed Eddie Gray to take the ball away from him. Fortunately, he was able to atone for his error and managed to win the ball back, and Kenny Burns cleared. Forest attacked again. Frank Clark's free-kick was flicked on to Bowyer by Withe, and it took a great interception by Trevor Cherry to prevent a goal attempt; the England man prodding the ball back to Stewart. In the Reds' next raid, Robbo received the ball from Gemmill's quick free-kick, and sped into the box past Paul Madeley, who unceremoniously brought the winger crashing to the ground. Even though the ball looked to be running out of play, surely, it must be a penalty. The ref said no penalty. Burns and Lloyd chased the official halfway up the pitch to protest, but it made no difference.

'Lucky' Leeds knew they been let off the hook, but decided that another goal was needed. They attacked in force. Hampton's floated centre was headed down to Flynn by Hankin, but the little Welshman rifled his shot past the woodwork. On the hour, Forest thought they had scored, when Withe headed down, Bowyer swept the ball into the Leeds net. Unfortunately, the Brummie ref ruled that Withe had jumped into Stewart as they had jumped to meet Barrett's corner, and the goal was disallowed. Five minutes later, came a genuine Reds goal.

Nottingham Forest v. Leeds United

Frank Clark picked the ball up near the halfway line and raced up the left, beat Currie and pulled the ball back from the byline for Withe to steer it past Stewart for the equaliser. This was Forest's number nine's first goal since 25 February. Now Forest and Withe in particular, threw everything at Leeds in an attempt to get the winner. Paul Hart got to Robbo's cross a split-second before the Forest front man, and then Stewart saved Withe's shot, before Barrett tried his luck. Turning Cherry, the full-back couldn't manage to bring the ball under control, and the danger was cleared. Gemmill swapped positions with Bowyer, as Forest tried to unsettle Leeds, who now looked happy to settle for a draw. Withe got himself booked for an innocuous foul on Currie; even the Leeds player told the ref it wasn't a bookable offence.

With time running out, a draw was looking the most likely result. Forest's final attack came from another of Robbo's crosses, as you might expect. Larry Lloyd glanced the ball to Bowyer, who was forced wide by Leeds' massed defenders, and the brief chance disappeared. Well, at least Forest maintained their unbeaten run at home.

The top of the League table now looked like this:

	PLD	W	D	L	F	A	PTS
Forest	**36**	**23**	**10**	**3**	**64**	**22**	**56**
Everton	39	21	10	8	69	42	52
Arsenal	38	19	10	9	56	32	48
Liverpool	36	20	7	9	53	32	47
Man City	37	18	10	9	66	44	46
Coventry	39	18	10	11	73	58	46

A stalwart of Forest's defence, centre-back **Larry Lloyd** joined Forest from Coventry in October 1976, firstly as an on-loan signing which subsequently became ratified, taking over Sammy Chapman's role at the heart of the Reds' defence. Born in Bristol on 6 October 1948, Lloyd became a firm favourite with the Forest fans, making 148 League appearances for the Nottingham Reds, scoring 6 goals. He had originally made his name with the other Reds, Liverpool, playing for them in their losing FA Cup final appearance against Arsenal in 1971. He didn't make Liverpool's final eleven for the 1974 cup final, when they beat Newcastle 3-0, but played for them in the 1972/73 Championship-winning side, also helping them to win the UEFA Cup in 1972/73. Larry won 4 full England caps, the first three between 1971 and 1972. His last was in 1980, in a 4-1 drubbing handed out by Wales at Wrexham. Big Larry was sold to Wigan Athletic in March 1981, where he became player-manager.

Nottingham Forest: Shilton, Barrett, Clark, McGovern, Lloyd, Burns, O'Neill, Gemmill, Withe, Bowyer, Robertson. Sub: Needham

Leeds United: Stewart, Madeley, Hampton, Flynn, Hart, Cherry, Gray F., Gray E., Hankin, Currie, Graham. Sub: Clarke

NOTTINGHAM FOREST v. QUEENS PARK RANGERS

Football League First Division, City Ground
Attendance: 30,339

Date: Tuesday 18 April 1978
Referee: Mr A.F. Jenkins (Scunthorpe)

Forest's fourth game of the season against QPR, the third at the City Ground, didn't manage to raise much excitement in the City, despite the inclusion of Dave Clement.

Forest made the early running and after only four minutes carved out the first real threat on goal. Peter Withe chased a lost cause to set up a chance for John McGovern, but the alert Phil Parkes dived to his right at full stretch to keep out the skipper's well-struck shot. Then it was Rangers' turn to provide the excitement. Paul McGee raced clear of Larry Lloyd on the edge of the area, however the young Irishman put the chance wide. Soon after, Stan Bowles showed his class with an exquisite pass that Leighton James couldn't quite reach. James was getting into some dangerous positions and again raced through to meet a long ball over the top of the Forest defence. It was end-to-end stuff, and this time it was Ian Bowyer who went close with a rifled shot that flashed narrowly past the post. Next, Peter Shilton had to be quick off his line to block Brian Williams as he was about to hit a cross from Paul Goddard. A minute before the half-hour mark Forest got their noses in front.

Colin Barrett drifted over a centre to Archie Gemmill who was floored from behind by Don Shanks. Despite being miles away from the incident, the referee didn't hesitate for a second. Penalty! Robertson placed the ball on the spot, clinically dispatching a firm shot wide of Phil Parkes' left hand. Rangers were still involved in the relegation battle and needed to take at least a point from this game, but weren't helped two minutes after the penalty when Bowles stupidly got himself booked for dissent; no doubt he was still unhappy with the decision. Stan Bowles' legendary short fuse often attracted a booking when he thought things weren't going his way.

The penalty spurred Forest back to the attack, with Ian Bowyer trying hard to add his name to the scoresheet. First, he almost got in a shot from Frank Clark's excellent pass, but was hustled out of it. Minutes later, he forced Parkes to make a diving save to keep out his fierce left-foot shot. Rangers' claims for a penalty of their own were turned away by Mr Jenkins, after Peter Shilton and Brian Williams had come together in a bone-crunching pile-up, in which fortunately neither was hurt. Just before the break, Williams had a half-chance presented to him when the ball ricocheted off Colin Barrett, however, the Manchester-born player was denied by a diving save from Shilton. Half-time: 1-0 to Forest.

At the start of the second half Forest had two gilt-edged opportunities to wrap the game up. Robbo picked the ball up on the left and sent in a lovely centre that Larry Lloyd headed over the bar. Then after a great three-man move involving Bowyer, O'Neill and Withe, the ball was played to Archie Gemmill, but sadly he cut across the ball and sliced his shot wide. Rangers hit back again, but this time despite Shilton making a great close-range save from McGee, the referee ruled that the young Irishman had strayed offside. John McGovern was having a great game and now whipped in a snap shot that Parkes did well to hold on to. Then when Peter Withe smashed in a rising drive, the former Walsall

---

Nottingham Forest 1
Robertson (penalty 29)

Queens Park Rangers 0

'keeper rose highest to punch the ball away. Moments later, Archie Gemmill floated a tempting cross into the area. Phil Parkes was beaten to the ball by Withe, but when it dropped invitingly for the Forest number nine, he snatched at his shot and the ball bounced clear off a Rangers defender.

A free-kick from Rangers caused a bit of a rumpus when Shilton was blocked out, but before any Rangers player could pounce, Mr Dependable, Frank Clark, was on hand to thump the ball away. Shortly after, the referee blew for time and Forest finished worthy winners of what had been a difficult game. The headlines proclaimed. 'Forest were cautious but they are Champions, you cannot deny it!' You certainly wouldn't want to bet against it!

Of the top six teams in the table, only Forest and Liverpool played in midweek, which gave them the chance to hoard away a few more points. Unfortunately for the Scousers, they could only manage a 2-2 at home to Ipswich.

The top of the League table looked like this:

	PLD	W	D	L	F	A	PTS
Forest	**37**	**24**	**10**	**3**	**65**	**22**	**58**
Everton	39	21	10	8	69	42	52
Arsenal	38	19	10	9	56	32	48
Liverpool	37	20	8	9	55	34	48
Man City	37	18	10	9	66	44	46
Coventry	39	18	10	11	73	58	46

Surely, Forest would be crowned Champions. Everton could still equal Forest's points total, providing they won their three remaining games, but it would take a miracle for them to beat the Reds' goal difference. Liverpool could get 59 points if they won their five remaining games. And, of course, in each of these scenarios, Forest would have to lose their last five games.

England drew 1-1 with Brazil in a friendly on 19 April 1978 at Wembley. England: Corrigan, Mills, Cherry, Greenhoff B., Watson, Currie, Keegan (Capt.), Coppell, Latchford, Francis, Barnes. Scorer: Keegan.
Brazil: Leao, Ze Maria, Abel, Amaral, Edinho, Cerezo, Rivelino, Dircue, Zico, Nunes (Batista), Gil. Scorer: Gil.

Well now! Things were looking decidedly hopeful. With games in hand, and six points clear, the League title was within Forest's reach. A win at the home of the Sky Blues might just do the trick, especially if the results of Forest's rivals were favourable – to the Reds, not them.

Nottingham Forest: Shilton, Barrett, Clark, McGovern, Lloyd, Burns, O'Neill, Gemmill, Withe, Bowyer, Robertson. Sub: O'Hare

Queens Park Rangers: Parkes, Clement, Gillard, Hollins, Howe, Shanks, Goddard, McGee, James L., Bowles, Williams. Sub: Cunningham

Forest's penalty king John Robertson.

COVENTRY CITY v. NOTTINGHAM FOREST

Football League First Division, Highfield Road
Attendance: 36,881

Date: Saturday 22 April 1978
Referee: Mr J. Bent (Hemel Hempstead)

Yet another clean sheet, this time against one of the highest scoring teams in the League. This match was billed as the goal getters versus the meanest defence. Unfortunately, on the day, both attacks proved to be a bit toothless. Surprising, considering that the Sky Blues' defence had been leaking goals with alarming regularity.

High-scoring Coventry welcomed back their big striker Mick Ferguson who returned for his first game since injuring an ankle against Leicester six weeks earlier. Prior to being injured Ferguson had scored 17 goals, and at one point was tipped to top the goalscoring charts for the season. However, missing the previous nine matches would rob him of this opportunity. Coventry's Scottish winger Tommy Hutchinson was forced to miss the match because of a bout of gastric flu. A depleted Forest side were defending their proud record of being unbeaten in their last twenty-first League outings. For this game, they would be without skipper John McGovern and Tony Woodcock, both suffering from groin strains, as well as the suspended Larry Lloyd.

In the opening minute, Green was booked for tripping Viv Anderson just outside the penalty area, but the free-kick came to nothing and Coventry were fortunate to escape. Coventry (who were in the hunt for a UEFA Cup place) hit back immediately, asking all sorts of questions of the Championship chasers' defence. Ferguson in particular was causing all manner of mayhem as he continually won the aerial battle with David Needham, setting up chance after chance for the rampant Sky Blues. The best of the bunch was a knock down that Scottish Under-21 international Ian Wallace hammered narrowly wide of Shilton's right-hand post, followed by a powerful header from former Leeds man Terry Yorath. John Beck swung over a corner from the right, which Yorath met at pace, his header hit Kenny Burns on the way to its target and deflected just wide of the upright.

Coventry continued to pressurise the Forest defenders, with route one proving to be an effective method. The ball was pumped up to Ferguson, and again the tall attacker headed down to Wallace. Fortunately for Forest the ginger-haired striker replicated his earlier effort by once again hitting a low shot a couple of yards wide. The combination of Ferguson and Wallace were giving Dave Needham and Footballer of the Year Kenny Burns a torrid afternoon.

Eventually, Forest managed to break out of defensive mode, and hit back with a long throw by Colin Barrett that might have produced more. The ball reached Robertson, who managed to fire the ball skywards towards Peter Withe. Sky Blues 'keeper Jim Blyth was quick to spot the danger and rushed out of his goal to smother the Forest striker's shot. Forest worked another good chance in the eighteenth minute, but when Robertson's corner reached Ian Bowyer, the number eight skied his shot over the bar. Coventry came back at the Reds, with Green only failing by a couple of inches to reach Ferguson's headed pass, which Anderson subsequently managed to nudge back to Shilton. Forest's goalkeeper was in action again immediately. This time, from Beck's right-wing cross he

Coventry City 0   Nottingham Forest 0

dived low to his left at full stretch to smother Ferguson's thrusting header. Then it was Jim Blyth's turn for action, diving low to take a stinging cross that would otherwise have reached the inrushing Peter Withe.

Again, the play swung back in Coventry's favour, but Alan Green sent his rising shot high into the Highfield Road terracing. In the thirty-sixth minute, it took an unbelievable save from Peter Shilton to keep the score at 0-0. Ian Wallace was sent away on the right, and took the ball round Barrett as the young full-back raced to meet him. Wallace lifted a slide-rule ball into the path of his strike partner. The big Sky Blues striker did everything right, he thought he had scored from only three yards out, but somehow Shilton managed to throw himself across goal to palm Ferguson's powerful header over the crossbar; an amazing save. Half-time: 0-0.

At the start of the second half, Forest swept onto the attack, and won a corner on the left, Robbo swung the ball over, but Ferguson sprang high to head the ball away. Back came Coventry, who knew that winning the extra point was vital if they were going to have any chance of making it into Europe next season. However, their opening raid was halted by the referee who penalised Wallace for foot up. The Sky Blues were not done yet, Shilton had to show his class with another breathtaking save to keep out Ferguson's fine effort. Then Terry Yorath took the ball away from Bowyer near the centre circle to set up Coventry's next attack. This ended with a shot from Alan Green that would probably have gone wide, although Shilton was taking no risks and took the ball cleanly.

Forest hit back with a penetrating run and cross by Colin Barrett that almost got through until Jim Holton stuck out a leg to divert the ball to safety. Referee Bent had so far kept a tight rein on the game, and now spoke to Kenny Burns after a minor infringement, further stamping his authority by booking Robbo for tripping Brian Roberts. Forest attacked again, and this time John O'Hare was unlucky to see his left-foot curler from outside the area slide past the angle of post and bar. The game swung back and forth, and now Shilton had to move smartly to whip away a centre before Ferguson could get his head to the ball. Seconds later, Alan Green hit a shot from just outside the box that had England's number-one goalkeeper diving to his right at full-stretch to make the catch.

Barry Powell was next to send in a cross aimed at Ferguson's head, but fortunately, Kenny Burns was in the right position to beat the big centre forward to the ball and head powerfully clear. Moments later, John Beck swung in another testing cross into the box, causing Shilton to charge off his line to gather the ball before it could reach Ferguson. The referee then found himself at the centre of two incidents, either of which might have won the game for Forest. In the first, Ian Bowyer wriggled his way into the area near the byline to create an opening for a shot, but before he could pull the trigger, he was bustled over by Roberts. The Forest players shouted for a penalty, but the referee shook his head; a dodgy decision some thought. Then not long after, Robbo went past Roberts and slid the ball to Archie Gemmill who went down in the box, looking distinctly like he'd been clumsily chopped down by Mick Coop. Forest's appeals were more vociferous this time, but again, the referee shook his head and waved play on. This was a bad decision, no doubt about it.

Kenny Burns had been outstanding all afternoon, and as Coventry threatened again when Powell looked like he might reach Wallace's header, Forest's commanding lynchpin again cleared the ball to safety. Then the ref blew for time.

COVENTRY CITY V. NOTTINGHAM FOREST

Coventry certainly had the better of this game, and based upon open play probably should have won. Mind you, Forest had those two serious calls for a penalty refused, the second of which looked to be clear cut, and of course if given, Forest would have won. Having said all of that, and the ref's decisions aside, it was the display of good goalkeeping and solid defending at both ends that really kept the scoresheet blank. Anyway, who cared about the lack of goals, this single point was enough to confirm Nottingham Forest as First Division Champions for the first time in their history.

Thousands of travelling Forest fans joined Brian Clough, Peter Taylor, and the players for a jubilant celebration that must have lasted a long time. It should have, and heaven knows they all deserved it, after achieving all that they had in this marvellous season.

Well, that was officially it! Forest couldn't be caught; they had won the League Championship for the first time in their history.

The top of the League table looked like this:

	PLD	W	D	L	F	A	PTS
Forest	**38**	**24**	**11**	**3**	**67**	**22**	**59**
Everton	40	21	11	8	69	42	53
Arsenal	39	20	10	9	59	33	50
Liverpool	38	21	9	8	58	34	50
Man City	38	19	10	9	70	45	48
Coventry	40	18	11	11	73	58	47

The two Merseyside clubs had given it their best shot, but in the end, it hadn't been good enough. Liverpool beat Norwich 3-0, and Everton drew 0-0 at Middlesbrough.

Hours after the Coventry game, Cloughie told the press that he and Taylor were already preparing for next season. They were looking to sign two players, and said that if they just got one of them they would win the title again. 'Ideally we want two. If we are successful in the transfer market with the big one, then we'll surprise everybody again.' Taylor's never-ending search for talented players had already taken him to Holland, so who they were talking about was a major topic in the pubs and clubs of Nottingham.

The new Champs didn't have much time to celebrate before they had to travel to East Anglia to meet Bobby Robson's Ipswich.

Coventry City: Blyth, Roberts, McDonald, Yorath, Holton, Coop, Green, Wallace, Ferguson, Powell, Beck. Sub: Thompson

Nottingham Forest: Shilton, Anderson, Barrett, O'Hare, Needham, Burns, O'Neill, Bowyer, Withe, Gemmill, Robertson. Sub: Clark

Ipswich Town v. Nottingham Forest

Football League First Division, Portman Road   **Date:** Tuesday 25 April 1978
Attendance: 30,062   **Referee:** Mr K.G. Salmon (Barnet)

Yet another clean sheet on their way to the title, Champions-elect Forest gave a very good Ipswich side a bit of a roasting at Portman Road. This was a game that would seriously change the record books, as stand-in striker Frank Clark eventually ended his career-long search for a League goal. Coming on at half-time as substitute for Peter Withe, Frank Clark eagerly grabbed his first ever League goal to cap a great Forest victory after Paul Mariner had popped in an own goal to put the Reds one up.

After a bit of to-ing and fro-ing in the opening quarter of an hour, it was Forest that almost took the lead. In the fifteenth minute, Ian Bowyer lifted the ball to Peter Withe who chested it down to Martin O'Neill, but unfortunately, the Irishman drove his shot straight into Cooper's arms. Then Robbo tricked his way past Burley and into the area, before drilling in a low shot that bounced out off a defender to Colin Barrett who was following up, but the full-back's shot was well taken by Paul Cooper in the Ipswich goal. Peter Shilton's first action of the game came when winger Clive Woods rounded Viv Anderson to whip in a low cross-cum-shot that the Forest 'keeper smothered before it could creep inside the post. Then just before the interval, John O'Hare leapt above Mariner and Whymark to head over his own bar for a corner that came to nothing. Half-time: 0-0.

For the second half Brian Clough changed Peter Withe for Frank Clark, a bit of an odd move to say the least, but Cloughie obviously knew more than the regular punter, because all of a sudden the Reds began to look much more menacing, zipping the ball around with power and pace. Nevertheless, it was the Forest 'keeper that was in action first. Ipswich found a bit of penetration and set up a chance for John Wark to test Shilton with a smart shot. Shilts was quickly in action again, this time to keep out a speculative shot from George Burley. After the impressive O'Hare had controlled the ball beautifully outside the area, he laid a clever pass to Barrett, whose shot on the turn beat the diving Cooper, to flash across goal and past the far post. Forest seemed to have the bit between their teeth and when Ian Bowyer won the ball in his own half, he sent Archie Gemmill racing clear from the halfway line. The Scottish international ripped in a rising shot from on the angle that Cooper managed to push away. Next, Frank Clark combined with Martin O'Neill to create a half-chance that the Ipswich defence managed to crowd out.

In the seventy-third minute, Colin Barrett's corner resulted in a calamity for Paul Mariner. The England striker had positioned himself in his own penalty area to help out his defence. But when the ball flew over the heads of both Dave Needham and Russell Osman, Mariner decided to lob the bouncing ball back to his goalkeeper. However, all he did was loft it over Cooper's outstretched arms and into the net off the upright. Oh dear!

Four minutes later, following Archie Gemmill's fabulous run through the Ipswich defence, 'Yer Man' was on hand to grab his moment of glory. Archie got the ball to John O'Hare, who exploded

---

Ipswich Town 0   **Nottingham Forest 2**

Mariner (73, own goal), Clark (78)

Ipswich Town v. Nottingham Forest

Peter Withe and Ipswich's Mick Mills watch as the ball spins away.

a ferocious shot that spun out off a defender to drop invitingly for Frank Clark, and although Frank was somewhat in uncharted waters he lashed it home with all the expertise of a top-class striker. His goal drew excited yells from all but the Ipswich players, their officials and fans, none of whom had any idea what the celebrations were all about. Frank's teammates surrounded him, burying him with their delight for his achievement. The congratulations went on for some time, and even Cloughie and the rest of the Forest bench were leaping around in excitement; the referee looked baffled by it all, but eventually restored calm and order.

Ipswich kicked off again and attempted to pull a goal back. They had a few chances in those final ten minutes. The first when John Wark blazed well wide, and later when Paul Mariner repeated the feat. Forest, happy as sandboys, played out the final few minutes to complete the double over Ipswich and savour what it would be like when the League Championship trophy was finally presented to them.

IPSWICH TOWN v. NOTTINGHAM FOREST

The top of the League table looked so beautiful:

	PLD	W	D	L	F	A	PTS
Forest	**39**	**25**	**11**	**3**	**67**	**22**	**61**
Everton	41	21	11	9	70	45	53
Liverpool	39	22	8	9	59	34	52
Man City	39	20	10	9	73	46	50
Arsenal	40	20	10	10	59	34	50
WBA	40	18	12	10	59	50	48

Leicester were still bottom, Newcastle one place above them, and Wolves had been sucked into the dogfight for First Division survival.

The new League Champions hardly had time for a rest before they were in action again. Their final home game of the season was against Birmingham, and of course, the Championship Trophy was to be presented to Forest prior to this game.

On the left wing of Forest's team throughout their marvellous run of trophy-winning was the great **John Robertson**, a genius of a footballer. Born Uddingston, near Glasgow on 20 January 1953, Robbo joined Forest as an apprentice straight from Scottish schoolboy football in May 1970. In his Forest career, he made 499 appearances, plus 15 as substitute, scoring 95 goals.

His career as a midfielder seemed to be going nowhere until he came under the influence of Brian Clough and Peter Taylor; they moved him out to the left wing. Robertson's 'stocky' build always reminded me of the legendary Ferenc Puskas. He wasn't bad was he? Both looked a bit slow, but looks can be deceptive. Both had an incredible burst of speed over a short distance, a good attribute for any footballer, but for a winger, it gave him the edge over the defender marking him at that moment. Show him the ball, slight feint, and away, sending in a stream of accurate and highly dangerous crosses. What Forest fan can forget the inch-perfect pass to the head of Trevor Francis that won the European Cup for Forest in the Olympic Stadium, Munich, on 30 May 1979, beating Malmo 1-0? A year later Robbo was the man that scored the vital goal against Kevin Keegan's highly fancied Hamburg to retain that coveted trophy. In June 1983 the by then manager of Derby Peter Taylor snatched him away from Cloughie's grasp for a spell at the Baseball Ground before returning to Forest in August 1985.

John won 28 caps for Scotland, scoring 8 goals. He played for the ill-fated Ally MacLeod's Scotland in one of their three games in the 1978 World Cup finals in Argentina, the disappointing 1-1 draw with Iran. Possibly, and I will repeat myself, he is best known for scoring the goal against Hamburg that won the European Cup for Forest in 1980. These days he is assistant manager to Martin O'Neill at Celtic.

Ipswich Town: Cooper, Burley, Mills, Talbot, Hunter, Osman, Osborne (Lambert), Wark, Mariner, Whymark, Woods.

Nottingham Forest: Shilton, Anderson, Barrett, O'Hare, Needham, Burns, O'Neill, Bowyer, Withe (Clark), Gemmill, Robertson.

Nottingham Forest v. Birmingham City

Football League First Division, City Ground
Attendance: 37,625

Date: Saturday 29 April 1978
Referee: Mr K. Walmsley (Blackpool)

A very noisy City Ground was heaving as Brian Clough and Peter Taylor, together with Jimmy Gordon, led out their triumphant first-team squad. New Champions Nottingham Forest were presented with the League Championship Trophy before this game with Birmingham City. Clough led the applause as skipper John McGovern stepped up to receive the trophy from Mr Jack Wiseman, vice-chairman of Birmingham City and member of the League Management Committee. Then Clough and his men saluted the capacity crowd, who in return gave them a standing ovation. Some say that it took over a week for the cheers to die down in the City of Nottingham. The Forest players did a lap of honour, resplendent in their tracksuits, showing off all their trophies to the crowd.

From a purist point of view, it's probably fair to say that the game itself was a little disappointing after the excitement of the presentation, but boy, it was still great! A thrilling contest in the best tradition of English football, contested by two teams that battled away for the entire match. Tony Woodcock returned after missing four games; however, he didn't last the full ninety minutes. The youngster limped from the field, to be replaced once more by Ian Bowyer. The Brummies put on a great show against the new League Champions in a tremendous action-packed game that was filled with all the elements that grace the English game. Birmingham's players could be excused for feeling a bit down, after putting in a performance that on another day would surely have earned them a couple of points. That they returned to St Andrew's with only one point was arguably down to one man, Peter Shilton. The England goalkeeper produced a series of breathtaking saves in an amazing display of agility and acrobatics.

The good-sized crowd were served a plate full of thrills and spills in this end-to-end game that at times resembled a cup tie. Forest's mean-spirited defence hadn't been put under this kind of pressure on many occasions, but at times this afternoon, the Blues boys gave them a right hammering. However, they failed to score. Mr Shilton saw to that.

In the first minute, the hearts of thousands of Forest's faithful fans missed a beat, when Terry Hibbitt whipped over left-wing centre that flew over Shilton's outstretched arms. Fortunately, Barrett was on hand to head the ball for a corner, the ball just missing the post. Then Trevor Francis neatly controlled the ball and ran at Forest's nervous-looking defence, but his low shot was deflected for another corner. This one was booted clear. In the next Blues attack, Francis made another good run down the right, latching on to an excellent through ball from Dillon, but on this occasion his swerving cross was headed away cleanly by Dave Needham. Just when it seemed that the Blues must score, Forest surprised the visitors with a lightening-fast break. A slip by Kevin Broadhurst presented Woodcock with a momentary clear sight of goal, but fortunately for the Blues, his fellow defenders managed to crowd the young striker out as he shaped to shoot.

Nottingham Forest 0   Birmingham City 0

NOTTINGHAM FOREST V. BIRMINGHAM CITY

In the twelfth minute, Broadhurst almost made amends for his error. He cleared a long ball, which Kenny Burns uncharacteristically mistimed, allowing the ball to bounce over his head into the run of Dillon, who sped towards Shilts; a goal seemed certain. Now cometh the Shilton show. In a demonstration of world-class goalkeeping, Shilts raced out to narrow the angle, and then gathered Dillon's shot with consummate ease. The Blues were tigerish in both midfield and defence, with the result that Forest were being pegged back in their own half. Finally, after a rare break, they managed to force a corner on the left, but the chance to get in a good cross was wasted. Then when Gallagher clearly fouled Robbo in the penalty area, Forest should have been awarded a spot kick, but for some reason the referee waved play on.

Forest were at last putting some nice passes together, and on the half-hour Jimmy Montgomery in the Birmingham goal was forced to make a brilliant save. Too clever by half, Terry Hibbitt back-heeled the ball into the run of O'Neill, who unleashed a cannonball of a shot that Montgomery could only parry for a corner. The Blues swung back to the attack, and Francis cut in from the right before firing over from a narrow angle. They were lucky to escape punishment in the thirty-fifth minute. Gallagher upended Gemmill near the edge of the area. Robbo took the free-kick, but could only throw up his hands in frustration as his curling shot hit the bar and went into the terraces.

The next free-kick went Blues' way after Needham had tripped Francis, but Dillon's shot was blocked. Minutes before half-time, Peter Withe squared a dangerous ball across the face of goal, but there was no one following up to put the ball in the net. Half-time: 0-0.

Bowyer replaced the injured Woodcock at half-time, and six minutes after the break, Trevor Francis set up a clear chance with a great defence-splitting ball to Calderwood, who was racing through the middle. It looked a goal all the way until Shilton sprinted off his line, and the now pressurised Calderwood shot straight into his arms. In the sixty-fourth minute the referee booked Gemmill for fouling Broadhurst. The Blues were beginning to get on top, but again it was that man Shilton who barred their way to goal. Following a right-wing corner from Steve Fox, Shilts kept out a Joe Gallagher shot with his knees. Then he was almost caught out by Trevor Francis, but recovered sufficiently to put the striker off, allowing Anderson to get in a timely block. Seconds later, the Forest 'keeper magnificently flew across goal to fist away a fierce long-range shot from Hibbitt.

Forest's defence was certainly under the cosh, and the Blues' next raid almost brought them a goal. Gallagher cleverly set up Francis, who whipped in a ferocious effort that Shilton couldn't have known much about until it bounced off his body. In the dying minutes, and against the run of play Forest nearly snatched the winner, however Montgomery brilliantly saved Bowyer's snap shot. Sadly, Woodcock's injury was to cause him to miss the final two games of a fantastic season.

Get the champagne out mother, Forest *are* League Champions.

The return friendly game against Derby County was played on Monday 1 May, Forest winning 2-1, with goals from McGovern and Withe.

Academic I know, but the top of the League table looked like this:

NOTTINGHAM FOREST v. BIRMINGHAM CITY

Forest's Ian Bowyer.

	PLD	W	D	L	F	A	PTS
Forest	**40**	**25**	**12**	**3**	**67**	**22**	**62**
Everton	42	22	11	9	76	45	55
Liverpool	40	23	8	9	61	34	54
Arsenal	41	21	10	10	60	34	52
Man City	40	20	11	9	74	47	51
WBA	41	18	13	10	60	51	49

On May Day, Liverpool hammered Manchester City 4-0 to move above their Merseyside rivals into second place in the League table.

Nottingham Forest: Shilton, Anderson, Barrett, McGovern, Needham, Burns, O'Neill, Gemmill, Withe, Woodcock (Bowyer), Robertson.

Birmingham City: Montgomery, Calderwood, Pendrey, Emmanuel, Gallagher, Broadhurst, Dillon, Francis, Bertschin, Hibbitt, Fox. Sub: Sbragia

West Bromwich Albion v. Nottingham Forest

Football League First Division, The Hawthorns
Attendance: 23,612

Date: Tuesday 2 May 1978
Referee: Mr C. Downey (Isleworth, Middlesex)

A dismal-sized crowd turned-up for this one, sixth-placed Albion versus Champions Forest. There really should have been more people at The Hawthorns, especially as it was the Baggies' final game of the season. The rain had turned the pitch into a bit of a paddy field, however the slippery surface made for some exciting stuff as both sides strove to control the greasy ball. Maybe the Albion groundstaff had done this deliberately in view of Baggies' forthcoming trip to play in China? Both teams played with the style and purpose with which they had graced this season's League competition.

The result might have been a bit academic; the final position in the League table of neither team could be affected, but you would never have thought so, the way the two sides went at each other. Forest went ahead in the sixteenth minute through Ian Bowyer. Tony Godden lost his footing as he moved to make a simple save, allowing a speculative shot from Colin Barrett to squirm out of his grasp, and there was the ginger-haired Bowyer to put it into the net. Albion stormed back onto the attack in the twenty-eighth minute, and after the ball had stuck to the pitch a few times, put together an exquisite three-man move that ended with a low twenty-five-yard cannonball from the 'Bomber' that picked up speed as it skimmed off the surface, literally flying into the net for the equaliser.

On thirty-five minutes, Regis outjumped the Forest defence to send in a neat header, which crashed against the underside of the bar. Unfortunately for the Reds, the ball came down inside the six-yard area, and there was young Wayne Hughes following up, to put the Baggies 2-1 ahead. A minute later and it was all-square again. There appeared to be more than a little confusion as to what the referee had blown for in a challenge that seemed more innocuous than anything else. Apparently, the ref felt that Brendan Batson had fouled Barrett, and of course, Robertson scored with a well-directed penalty. Then just before the break, Cunningham managed to wriggle his way into the Forest penalty area, only to be robbed of the ball before he could pull the trigger. Two apiece at half-time.

In the second half, Peter Shilton showed all of his class with two great saves. The first was an amazingly gymnastic effort to keep out a Tony 'Bomber' Brown thunderbolt. The second was an equal test of his elasticity, to prevent big Cyrille Regis from winning the game for Albion. The second half conditions did nothing to help the flow of this game, and it was a tribute to all of the players that they produced such a thrilling contest. For most of the half, Forest were second best to the Baggies in most of the play. They seemed to run out of steam, particularly in the middle of the park, where earlier they had competed so well. Not surprising really; after all, they were playing their third match in four days. Never mind, they put in a dogged performance to retain their unbeaten run. Now for Anfield to meet Liverpool.

West Bromwich Albion 2
Brown T. (28), Hughes (35)

Nottingham Forest 2
Bowyer (16), Robertson (penalty 36)

West Bromwich Albion v. Nottingham Forest

Peter Shilton grabs the ball under a serious challenge from Albion's forwards.

The top of the League table looked satisfyingly like this:

	PLD	W	D	L	F	A	PTS
Forest	**41**	**25**	**13**	**3**	**69**	**24**	**63**
Liverpool	41	24	8	9	65	34	56
Everton	42	22	11	9	76	45	55
Arsenal	41	21	10	10	60	34	52
Man City	41	20	11	10	74	51	51
WBA	42	18	14	10	62	53	50

One more game left in a gruelling but very satisfying and successful season. Off to Merseyside to meet the other Reds for the fourth time in the season.

West Bromwich Albion: Godden, Batson, Statham, Tony Brown, Wile, Robertson, Cantello, Robson B., Regis, Hughes, Cunningham. Sub: Martin
Nottingham Forest: Shilton, Anderson, Barrett, McGovern, Lloyd, Burns, O'Neill, Gemmill, Withe, Bowyer, Robertson. Sub: Clark

LIVERPOOL v. NOTTINGHAM FOREST

Football League First Division, Anfield
Attendance: 50,021

Date: Thursday 4 May 1978
Referee: Mr N.J. Ashley (Nantwich)

The final League game in a hectic season; first against second. Game number fifty-six for Forest, not counting friendlies. I suppose a draw was a fair result as neither team had anything to fight for, other than pride; third-placed Everton had already finished their fixtures.

The 1976/77 European and League Champions Liverpool had made a brave fight of chasing Forest all the way to the title, picking up 16 points out of a possible 18 since the beginning of April. Kenny Burns missed his only game of the season, after Brian Clough had given him the night off to travel to London's Café Royal to collect the Football Writer's Association Award: 1977/78 Footballer of the Year. Skipper John McGovern passed a fitness test despite earlier doubts concerning his ongoing groin strain. Tony Woodcock would have to sit out the final game of the season, Ian Bowyer again getting the nod for the number ten shirt.

Liverpool's top scorer Kenny Dalglish, an ever-present in their League games, had scored 20 goals in his first season in English football, but none against Forest; no doubt he would be trying hard to get one in this game, especially as he had banged in a hat-trick against Manchester City three days earlier. In all competitions this season, Dalglish scored a total of 27 goals.

The manner with which Forest extracted a draw at Anfield gave rise to the thought that this game had been treated as an exercise in the kind of defensive football that the Reds would need to employ in next season's European Cup. Forest absorbed and nullified Liverpool's attacking flair in a wonderful demonstration of 'away-leg' tactics, and in the end the Scousers seemed to have run out of attacking ideas. For a time Liverpool's players must have been pleased not to be facing the brilliance of young Chris Woods, that is, until they remembered that it would be Peter Shilton who would be providing tonight's ultimate barrier. Mind you, they had beaten Shilton once this season. However, there was no way that Shilton was about to allow Ray Clemence to upstage him by grabbing the next day's headlines in any way whatsoever.

Likewise Larry Lloyd, once an Anfield favourite. The former darling of the Kop was as steady as a rock at the heart of a Forest defence weakened on paper at least by the absence of the marvellous Kenny Burns, Lloyd produced the kind of forceful determination that had become his trademark. The whole team were heroes on the night that Forest extended their incredible unbeaten run in the League to an amazing 26 games to end the season at the top of the First Division table by a staggering seven-point margin from nearest rivals Liverpool. There was no way Forest were going to allow Liverpool to beat them. Remember, the Scousers had only managed to score one goal against the League's meanest defence in 570 minutes of football.

In the seventh minute of this absorbing game, Liverpool forced a corner. Dalglish's kick evaded the massed ranks of defenders and attacked alike to end up at the feet of Ray Kennedy. But before the former Arsenal striker could pull the trigger, Peter Shilton dived bravely to smother the danger.

Liverpool 0   Nottingham Forest 0

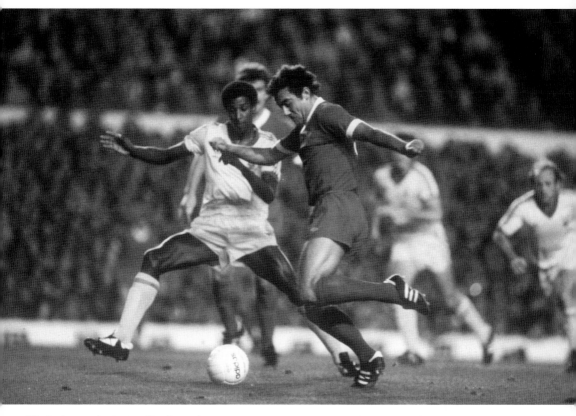

Viv Anderson tries to stop Ray Kennedy.

Forest were finding it difficult to create much in the way of openings, but nearly got through in the fifteenth minute, after a piece of skill from John Robertson. Archie Gemmill sent his Scottish countryman away on the left, before whipping in a low cross that Withe cleverly left to set up the briefest sight of goal, but unfortunately Alan Hansen recovered in time to prod the ball behind for a corner. So far, Ray Clemence hadn't had much to do, and again it was his rival for the England goalkeeping shirt that was called into action first. Kenny Dalglish zipped in a quick free-kick that Shilton smothered by flinging himself at David Fairclough's feet.

Moments later, Forest thought they had scored when Larry Lloyd headed home Archie Gemmill's curling corner, but Forest's centre-back was penalised for impeding Ray Clemence. Soon after this let-off for Liverpool, Archie Gemmill had sent Robbo away on the left and Forest's World Cup winger tricked his way past Phil Neal. Peter Withe launched himself at the ball, but headed narrowly wide. With half-time approaching, Shilton made the best save of the match thus far. Dalglish fooled Colin Barrett before crashing in a low shot that incredibly Shilts managed to push away after seemingly turning in midair. Half-time: 0-0.

Liverpool, no doubt smarting badly at having lost their League title plus the League Cup final to Forest, now threw everything they had at their usurpers. Likewise, Forest drew on all their vast

LIVERPOOL V. NOTTINGHAM FOREST

reserves of calmness and patience, and having weathered an early onslaught might have scored. Following a clever piece of work from Peter Withe, the ball was played to John McGovern who volleyed narrowly wide of Clemence's post.

Ray Kennedy caused a mild flutter in a few Forest hearts when he controlled a through pass superbly. However, like McGovern's effort, his final shot flashed wide. Peter Shilton was at his confidence-building best, his positional play and handling of the ball quite brilliant. Only once did the Forest 'keeper give Liverpool any encouragement. That was when Emlyn Hughes drilled in a low shot that skidded off the slick surface to bounce up awkwardly at Shilts as he attempted to gather. The ball leaked from his grasp into the path of the inrushing Dalglish, but before the Scot could do anything Shilton dived at his feet to push the ball away, and Frank Clark thumped it towards Row Z.

After that little bit of excitement, the players seemed to sense that it was pretty much all over. Minutes later the referee's whistle signalled the end of the game, and a memorable season for Nottingham Forest. Brian Clough and Peter Taylor, the players and the backroom staff at Forest could now officially relax and bathe in the sunshine of their remarkable achievements. They had won the coveted League Championship in style, as well as the Football League Cup. A season to remember indeed.

The top of the League table looked like this:

	PLD	W	D	L	F	A	PTS	
Forest	**42**	**25**	**14**	**3**	**69**	**24**	**64**	**CHAMPIONS**
Liverpool	42	24	9	9	65	34	57	
Everton	42	22	11	9	76	45	55	
Arsenal	41	21	10	10	60	34	52	
Man City	41	20	11	10	74	51	51	
WBA	42	18	14	10	62	53	50	

Arsenal still had to play the Rams at the Baseball Ground on 9 May, after they had met Ipswich in the FA Cup final on 6 May. Manchester City's final fixture was at Chelsea on 5 May, the game ending in a 0-0 draw.

Liverpool: Clemence, Neal, Hansen, Thompson P., Kennedy, Hughes, Dalglish, Case, Fairclough, McDermott, Souness. Sub: Callaghan

Nottingham Forest: Shilton, Anderson, Barrett, McGovern, Lloyd, Clark, O'Neill, Gemmill, Withe, Bowyer, Robertson. Sub: Needham

Postscript

In the FA Cup final on 6 May, Ipswich surprised many people by beating Arsenal 1-0 to win the FA Cup for the first time. And finally, on Tuesday 9 May, Derby beat Arsenal 3-0 with goals from Gordon Hill, Colin Chesters and Terry Curran.

Great news for Forest fans on the international scene with Ally MacLeod selecting Burns, Gemmill and Robertson in his Scotland squad for the 1978 World Cup finals in Argentina.

Six days after entertaining Forest, on 10 May 1978, Liverpool beat Bruges 1-0 at Wembley to retain the European Cup. Forest had not only prevented Liverpool from retaining the League title, but also from winning a hat-trick of consecutive League titles.

So that was it, Nottingham Forest were officially crowned Champions of England. Forest had played the best and had beaten the best. Out of 42 League games, they had won 25, drawn 14, and had only been beaten on 3 occasions, all away from home, thus winning the Championship a full seven points ahead of runners-up Liverpool. They were unbeaten in the League since 19 November 1977 which spanned a full 26 games.

In the FA Cup, they had played 6 games, drawing twice, and losing only once. In the Football League Cup, they had triumphed; playing 8 games, winning all but one, and that was a draw.

A truly remarkable record in all domestic competitions of: played 56, won 35, drawn 17, lost 4, in the process scoring 104 goals and conceding only 36.

Two trophies in their first season back in the top flight was beyond everyone's wildest dreams. Next season would see Nottingham Forest play in the European Champions Cup for the first ever time – A season to remember indeed.

So, that was Forest's first Championship-winning season. The following season they qualified for the 1978/79 European Champion's Cup, and as we know, they triumphed, beating Malmo 1-0 in the final with a Trevor Francis goal. They also retained the Football League Cup, beating Southampton 3-2. The Reds finished the League programme in the runners-up spot, and won the FA Charity Shield on 12 August 1978 by walloping cup winners Ipswich Town 5-1 at Wembley. The year after this, 1979/80, Forest retained the European Champion's Cup when they beat Hamburg, again by the score of 1-0, courtesy of a John Robertson goal.

The Players

Peter Shilton MBE, CBE – **goalkeeper** – 37 League appearances; 6 appearances in the FA Cup.

John Middleton – **goalkeeper** – 5 League appearances; 1 appearance in the Football League Cup.

Chris Woods – **goalkeeper** – 7 appearances in the Football League Cup.

Viv Anderson – **right-back** – 37 League appearances, 3 goals; 5 appearances in the FA Cup; 8 appearances in the Football League Cup, 1 goal.

Colin Barrett – **full-back** – 33 League appearances, plus 2 as substitute, 1 goal; 3 appearances in the FA Cup; 5 appearances in the Football League Cup.

Frank Clark – **left-back** – 12 League appearances, plus 1 as substitute, 1 goal; 3 appearances in the FA Cup; 4 appearances in the Football League Cup.

John McGovern – **midfield** – 31 League appearances, 4 goals; 4 appearances in the FA Cup; 7 appearances in the Football League Cup, 1 goal.

Larry Lloyd – **centre-back** – 26 League appearances; 2 appearances in the FA Cup; 6 appearances in the Football League Cup, 1 goal.

Kenny Burns – **centre-back** – 41 League appearances, 4 goals; 6 appearances in the FA Cup; 8 appearances in the Football League Cup.

Dave Needham – **centre-back** – 16 League appearances, 4 goals; 6 appearances in the FA Cup.

Martin O'Neill – **right midfield** – 38 League appearances, plus 2 as substitute, 8 goals; 6 appearances in the FA Cup, 2 goals; 8 appearances in the Football League Cup, 3 goals.

Archie Gemmill – **midfield** – 32 League appearances, plus 2 as substitute, 3 goals; 4 appearances in the FA Cup.

Ian Bowyer – **midfield** – 25 League appearances, plus 3 as substitute, 4 goals; 3 appearances in the FA Cup; 8 appearances in the Football League Cup, 6 goals.

John Robertson – **left midfield/wing** – 42 League appearances, 12 goals (6 penalties); 6 appearances in the FA Cup, 3 goals (1 penalty); 8 appearances in the Football League Cup, 3 goals (2 penalties).

Peter Withe – **striker** – 40 League appearances, 12 goals; 6 appearances in the FA Cup, 2 goals; 8 appearances in the Football League Cup, 5 goals.

Tony Woodcock – **striker** – 36 League appearances, 11 goals; 6 appearances in the FA Cup, 4 goals; 8 appearances in the Football League Cup, 4 goals.

John O'Hare – **striker** – 10 League appearances; 1 substitute appearance in the FA Cup; 1 appearance in the Football League Cup, plus 1 as substitute, 1 goal.

Clough & Taylor: The 'Dynamic Duo'

The Dynamic Duo first met at Middlesbrough when a young Brian Clough was introduced to Boro goalkeeper Peter Taylor, and during the time until Clough was transferred to Sunderland in July 1961, the two became friends. In the summer of 1965, Brian Clough was looking after the youth side at Sunderland and Peter Taylor was managing non-League Burton Albion when Clough was offered the manager's job at Hartlepool United. The rest, as they say, is history.

Brian Clough OBE, MA – manager

'Brian Clough walks on water.' A claim made about only a handful of people since those early days of Christianity in Galilee. Brian Clough was one of those few!

This great centre forward, whose career was sadly cut short through injury, moved into football management at Hartlepool United, staying until 1967 when he took over the reigns of struggling Second Division outfit Derby County. By the end of the following season, Derby fans were celebrating Derby's Second Division Championship win. Then in 1971/72 Derby were crowned Champions of the First Division, Leeds having been denied the 'double' that season courtesy of a last-game-of-the-season defeat at the hands of Wolverhampton Wanderers, amid allegations of attempted match-fixing.

Never short of an opinion, Clough outraged the FA after criticising them for not taking the severest action possible against Leeds United and their poor disciplinary record, and then upset some of his own players at Derby, calling them cheats, and claiming they hadn't given of their all in a game because they had one eye on the forthcoming England World Cup qualifying game against Poland. Derby chairman Sam Longston told his manager to shut up. Clough and his assistant Peter Taylor resigned, reputedly hoping that the Derby board would back down; they didn't. Instead, they appointed Dave Mackay as manager. Next port of call for Clough and Taylor was Third Division Brighton and Hove Albion, although Cloughie left to join Leeds in July 1974 after only eight months in charge.

Brighton chairman Mike Bamber was furious that Clough had decided to desert his club after such a short time in charge. There were accusations and counter-accusations, with writs and threats of more writs, and broken compensation agreements. The whole episode was a sad indictment of the shenanigans that went on in English football. However, compared to the great man's next appointment, the Brighton saga was tame to say the least. Brian Clough's forty-four stormy days at Leeds United ended in his sacking by chairman Manny Cussins and the United board.

Upon his arrival at Elland Road, where he was seen by many at the club to be the ideal man to bring back the great days they had enjoyed under the tutelage of Don Revie, Clough ran into a set of established stars that seemed not to appreciate his appointment one little bit, a claim subsequently strongly refuted by the Leeds players.

Clough introduced a number of unpopular disciplinary measures considered by many to be draconian and ill conceived, at the same time placing some of the senior players on the transfer list. A run of six defeats in the League saw United, (a not at all accurate term to describe the prevailing situation at the football club – disunited would be more accurate), slip to nineteenth in the League. Obviously, the Leeds fans were not too impressed. They turned on Clough, barracking him at every opportunity. This must have been an awful time for Brian Clough. Leeds United were a giant amongst English football clubs, and had he been allowed to get on with the job in his own way, there is no doubt that he would have brought Leeds the success they hungered for. Still, their loss was Forest's gain.

One of the few managers to have won the League Championship with two different football clubs, Brian Clough strode through three decades of English football. The greatest manager never to manage the England football team, despite being overwhelmingly the people's choice. And he was, a man of the people, a hero from the working classes, who seemed to court controversy, and thrive on it.

Born in Middlesbrough on 21 March 1935, this young man made his name as a centre forward with Middlesbrough and Sunderland, famous for his phenomenal goalscoring prowess. Playing for Second Division Middlesbrough, Clough was the leading goalscorer in season 1958/59.

In season 1959/60, on the back of his scoring feats for Boro, he was selected for the Football League side to play the Irish League in Belfast of 23 September 1959, making an indelible mark on the game by scoring all five goals in a 5-0 victory. Obviously everyone was impressed, particularly the England selectors. He was chosen at centre forward for England's Home International Championship game against Wales at Ninian Park in Cardiff on 17 October 1959, England's first game following the retirement of Billy Wright. Sadly for Clough, he failed to shine in a 1-1 draw. England's only goal was scored by Jimmy Greaves. Eleven days later, 28 October, Clough won his second and last England cap, against Sweden at Wembley. England lost 3-2, their goals coming from John Connelly and Bobby Charlton. The selectors felt that that there was little mileage in the Clough and Greaves partnership, and for the next England game, poor Brian was dropped, Hibernian's Joe Baker being selected in his place. Clough still scored 39 League goals for Middlesbrough that season. With a centre forward as prolific as Brian Clough Boro really should have won promotion to the top flight. The team's problems stemmed from their inability to plug the holes in their leaky defence. The best they achieved was two fifth-place finishes in Cloughie's last two seasons with them.

At the start of the 1961/62 season, Clough moved to Sunderland – again, and somewhat surprisingly, a Second Division outfit – for a reported fee of £42,000. He had scored 197 goals in 213 League games for Boro, 204 goals in 222 games in all competitions. In his first season at Roker Park Clough hit 29 goals in 34 League games for the Black Cats, missing out on promotion to Division One by one point. In all competitions that season, he netted 34 times in 43 games.

Brian Clough was a goal-scoring sensation, of that there was no doubt. In 274 League appearances, he scored 251 goals, almost a goal a game, before being cruelly cut down with a serious knee injury on Boxing Day 1962 in Sunderland's 3-2 defeat by Bury at Roker Park. After missing the entire 1963/64 season, at the end of which Sunderland won promotion to Division One, he was ready to make his comeback at the start of the following campaign. Unfortunately, Clough only managed 3 games and 1 goal before being forced to retire from the playing side of the game at the age of twenty-nine. And yes, we know it was a different game in his playing days, slower and more thoughtful, but you still had to put the ball in the back of the net, with some of the world's best and hardest trying to stop you. His overall playing record in all competitions is 267 goals in 296 appearances – an average of one goal every 1.1 games.

After one disappointing season following a glittering managerial career spanning from 1965 to 1993, Brian Clough retired from football on 26 April 1993. Two League Championships, two European Cups and four League Cups, among other trophies, was not a bad haul.

Unpredictable, confident to the extreme, focused, concentrated and passionate. Undoubtedly one of the finest strikers and managers the game of football has ever known; a truly great man.

Brian Clough OBE, MA sadly passed away on 20 September 2004.

Peter Taylor – assistant manager

Wily fox Peter Taylor was the calming influence that Brian Clough needed. Born in Nottingham, on 2 July 1928, Taylor made 86 League appearances in goal for Coventry City, signing for the Sky Blues in May 1946, after being on Forest's books as an amateur. In August 1955, he was transferred to Middlesbrough, where he made 140 League appearances, before moving to Port Vale in June 1961, playing in only 1 League game. He subsequently joined Southern League Burton Albion. It was at Middlesbrough that Taylor first met Brian Clough, the old stager and the young pretender becoming firm friends.

In October 1962, Taylor became manager of Burton Albion, winning the Southern League Cup with the Eton Park club in 1963/64. In October 1965, Clough persuaded Taylor to join him at Hartlepool as his assistant, and from there to Second Division Derby County in June 1967, where they won promotion as Second Division Champions in 1968/69, and their first League Championship in 1971/72, reaching the semi-finals of the European Cup the following season.

The duo resigned in October 1973, and a month later Taylor followed Clough to Brighton as assistant manager. Taylor took over as manager of Brighton in June 1974 when Cloughie took the ill-fated 44-day long Leeds job, guiding the Seagulls to fourth spot in the Third Division in 1975/76. Peter Taylor once again joined his long-time partner in July 1976 at Nottingham Forest. Another trophy-laden period followed, ending when Taylor announced his retirement at the end of the 1981/82 season.

At Wembley on 17 March 1979, Peter Taylor proudly led out the Forest team for the 1979 Football League Cup Final, in which Forest beat Southampton 3-2. Subsequently, Peter Taylor returned to football management on 11 August 1982 with Second Division Derby County. After Taylor poached John Robertson in 1983 whilst Cloughie was away on one of his charitable fund-raising trips, walking the Pennine Way, the relationship between the one-time partners and friends dipped into a stubborn feud that sadly never ended.

Peter Taylor left Derby on 4 April 1984, and the Rams were relegated at the end of that 1983/84 season. The world of football lost one of its characters when Peter Taylor died in his Majorcan Villa in October 1990.

Other titles published by Tempus

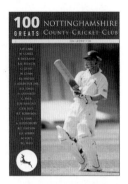

Nottinghamshire County Cricket Club 100 Greats
JIM LEDBETTER

Featuring 100 of the greatest players to have represented Nottinghamshire over their 180-year history, this book recalls the glory days of the club and celebrates the talents and achievements of its finest batsmen, bowlers, wicketkeepers and all-rounders right up to the present day. Jim Ledbetter is a lifelong Nottinghamshire supporter and chairman of the Association of Cricket Statisticians and Historians.
0 7524 2745 8

Nottingham Pubs
DOUGLAS WHITWORTH

This book is a fascinating record of 200 of Nottingham's public houses past and present. In addition to the most historic hostelries, it also records many of the backstreet pubs which disappeared in the 1970s when whole districts of the city were cleared. This collection of archive images will be of interest to both those who frequent the city's pubs and all those who are interested in the history of Nottingham.
0 7524 3243 5

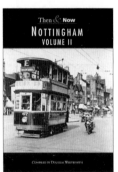

Nottingham Then & Now Volume II
DOUGLAS WHITWORTH

This second volume of comparative photographs by local historian Douglas Whitworth shows the many changes that took place in Nottingham during the nineteenth and twentieth centuries. It covers many districts of the city, showing humble cottages and architectural masterpieces, and the city centre in the days of Nottingham's first electric tram system. These photographs magnificently illustrate the great transformations the city has seen.
0 7524 3100 5

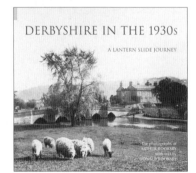

Derbyshire in the 1930s A Lantern Slide Journey
ARTHUR ROOKSBY AND DONALD ROOKSBY

The photographs in this book are the work of Arthur Rooksby, an amateur photographer who used them for lantern slide shows in church halls around the county. Full of stunning views of the Derbyshire countryside and accompanied by text supplied by Rooksby's son, this book takes the reader through some of the most scenic parts of 1930s Derbyshire.
0 7524 3258 3

If you are interested in purchasing other books published by Tempus, or in case you have difficulty finding any Tempus books in your local bookshop, you can also place orders directly through our website
www.tempus-publishing.com